DATE DUE

¿de Veras?

Mary Burritt
Christiansen
Poetry Series

MARY BURRITT CHRISTIANSEN POETRY SERIES
V. B. PRICE, SERIES EDITOR

Also available in the University of New Mexico Press Mary Burritt Christiansen Poetry Series:

Poets of the Non-Existent City: Los Angeles in the McCarthy Era
edited by Estelle Gershgoren Novak

Selected Poems of Gabriela Mistral edited by Ursula K. Le Guin

Deeply Dug In by R. L. Barth

Amulet Songs: Poems Selected and New by Lucile Adler

In Company: An Anthology of New Mexico Poets After 1960
edited by Lee Bartlett, V. B. Price, and Dianne Edenfield Edwards

Tiempos Lejanos: Poetic Images from the Past by Nasario García

Refuge of Whirling Light by Mary Beath

The River Is Wide/El río es ancho: Twenty Mexican Poets, a Bilingual Anthology
edited and translated by Marlon L. Fick

A Scar Upon Our Voice by Robin Coffee

CrashBoomLove: A Novel in Verse by Juan Felipe Herrera

In a Dybbuk's Raincoat: Collected Poems by Bert Meyers

Rebirth of Wonder: Poems of the Common Life by David M. Johnson

Broken and Reset: Selected Poems, 1966 to 2006 by V. B. Price

The Curvature of the Earth by Gene Frumkin and Alvaro Cardona-Hine

Derivative of the Moving Image by Jennifer Bartlett

Map of the Lost by Miriam Sagan

A Bigger Boat: The Unlikely Success of the Albuquerque Poetry Slam Scene edited by Susan McAllister, Don McIver, Mikaela Renz, and Danny Solis

¿de Veras?

Young Voices from the National Hispanic Cultural Center

Edited by **MIKAELA JAE RENZ**

and **SHELLE VANETTEN-LUACES**

Foreword by V. B. Price

University of New Mexico Press
Albuquerque

Printed in the United States of America
12 11 10 09 08 1 2 3 4 5

Library of Congress Cataloging-in-Publication Data

De veras? : young voices from the National Hispanic Cultural Center / edited by Mikaela Jae Renz and
Shelle VanEtten-Luaces ; foreword by V. B. Price.
p. cm. — (Mary Burritt Christiansen poetry series)
ISBN 978-0-8263-4359-8 (cloth : alk. paper)
1. American poetry—Hispanic American authors.
2. Hispanic Americans—Poetry.
3. American poetry—New Mexico.
4. Teenagers' writings, American.
I. Renz, Mikaela Jae, 1975-
II. VanEtten-Luaces, Shelle.
III. National Hispanic Cultural Center of New Mexico.
PS591.H58D4 2008
811'.54080868—dc22
2007047489

Designed and typeset by Mina Yamashita.
Text composed in Utopia Std, a typeface designed by Robert Slimbach for Adobe in 1989.
Display composed in Frutiger 77 Black Condensed, designed by Adrian Frutiger in 1976.
Printed by Thomson-Shore, Inc. on 55# Natures Natural.

To the creative voice

that resides within each student

represented on these pages—

may you speak, sing, and scream

throughout the years.

Contents

Foreword by V. B. Price / xiii

Preface by Mikaela Jae Renz / xix

Invocation by Tamara Bryan / xxiii

2002 / 1

AMBROSE VIGIL
Hard Times / 3

ANISHA IMHOFF-KERR
What makes me / 4

ANTHONY ROYBAL
I Came . . . / 5

ASHLEY M. ELLISON
Broken Pieces / 6

CARLOS CONTRERAS
Human Zoo / 7

DAMIEN FLORES
Asphalt Memories / 9

EHREN SALAZAR-MARCRUM
Icons / 11

ELICIA CARDENAS
Mi cultura es Mexicana / 12

JASMINE SENA
Crush / 13

JEREMY MAES
Three dead rattlesnakes hung / 14

KATE TWITCHELL
I am white / 15

KEVIN PACHECO
La Llorona / 17

KHAMYRA A. HALL
Brown and Proud / 18

MARCELO MOYA
Preparation for the Future / 20

MARISOL SERVIZIO / KHAMYRA A. HALL
Imprisonment / 21

MATTHEW LUCERO
True Wealth / 23

REBECCA ORTEGA
Denim Jeans: An American Icon / 24

SAMANTHA EMORD
The Tower / 25

SARA HUMPHREYS
Revelation / 26

MIKAELA JAE RENZ
***El Té,* Alfredo Ceibal, 1986 / 27**

SHELLE VANETTEN-LUACES
The Problem with Males and Art / 29

2003 / 31

AMBROSE VIGIL
Shadows of Death and Last Breaths / 33

ANISHA IMHOFF-KERR
That Person Is Me / 34

ASHLEY M. ELLISON
I was partially insane from all the drugs I took / 38

CARLOS ANDERSON
Silence is sometimes the best answer / 39

CARLOS CONTRERAS
You / 40

DEMI OLIVAS
Beauty to Pieces / 42

EGLA LÓPEZ
Remorse / 48

EHREN SALAZAR-MARCRUM
Insomniac / 49

FELICIA HERRERA
She said she wanted to leave the country and explore the sky / 50

GRACIELA GONZALES
New Mexico / 51

JASMINE SENA
Soak up a sudden or violent / 52

JEREMY MAES
Isms / 54

NAKYA ELY-WEST
Misused Toys / 56

NIKKI POINDEXTER
The Land of Enchantment / 57

PENNY CHIMAL
When Elk Hooves Chatter / 59

REVÉ CHEWIWI
La Chola / 60

SAMANTHA EMORD
Writing Pains / 61

SAMANTHA INNIS
He Was, She Was, They Were / 63

MIKAELA JAE RENZ
Connect the dots / 64

SHELLE VANETTEN-LUACES
I'm Two / 66

2004 / 69

AMBROSE VIGIL
For the Love of Hip Hop / 71

BRITTANY JEWEL
Puppet Strings / 73

CHASITY A. VIGIL
Intolerance / 74

DEMI OLIVAS
Vanity / 76

GRACIELA GONZALES
Emotions that Come with Death and War / 78

GREGORIO GARCIA
Creation / 80

ISAIAH BACA
Monja Coronada / 81

JASMINE SENA
Paper napkins are no place / 82

JENNIFER OTERO
Where I Come From / 84

KALY THAYER
Three Guys in My Neighborhood / 85

LAUREN BADUA
Mezcal Circle / 87

PAUL S. HOEG
Green Chile Stew / 90

ROBYN RUFF-WAGNER
Fear / 91

SAMANTHA INNIS
Bleed Through / 93

SONJA CHACON
no one noticed the night / 94

STEPHEN JUAREZ
Better Days / 96

TAMARA BRYAN
Origins / 97

MIKAELA JAE RENZ
Sister Space / 99

SHELLE VANETTEN-LUACES
My Life in 142 Words / 102

2005 / 103

ALAN HOTCHKISS
Aztec Sunrise / 105

ALICIA LEGER
My Voice / 106

ANA ROMERO
Soldados / 108

DEMI OLIVAS
American "Lover"? / 109

EMILIO JURI
Argentina / 111

JULIAN GODINEZ
What You See Is Me / 114

MARY FERGUSON
Loco L.A. / 115

NICK ETRE
Another Four Years of Fear / 116

SAMANTHA INNIS
Hello, New York / 118

MIKAELA JAE RENZ
Peddling in Barelas / 119

SHELLE VANETTEN-LUACES
What's New / 121

2006 / 123

ALYSSA GARCIA
I want to tell them everything that happened that first night I didn't come home / 125

ANTHONY "WONDERBOY" ALANIZ
My America / 127

ANTONIO RAEL
La Muerte de un Loco / 128

BIANCA LOPEZ
I carry the bones of my brother that have not yet, nor will they ever, change / 130

CARLOS CONTRERAS
Common ground / 131

DEMI OLIVAS
Starlight quivers between / 134

ELISSA HUTSON
Childhood / 137

ESMÉ VAANDRAGER
Two Voices: Hendrik, Esmé. / 138

FAUSTINO VILLA
My reasons to live are not so big / 141

JESSE JAMES
I should've danced stronger / 142

JOE ROMERO
Abuela, I'm sorry for forgetting / 143

JULIO MENDEZ / SARA SAMANI
Writing a New Book / 145

LAUREN BRENNER
Ode to My Bed / 147

LENELL STOREY
This is home / 148

MARTÍN MONTAÑO-PILCH
Innocence / 151

MATTHEW MEYER
The Average High / The Academy Was . . . / 153

ROBERT P. RAMIREZ
Twelve Voices / 155

SAMANTHA INNIS
Anatomy / 158

SARA SAMANI
She carries the white stick / 160

MIKAELA JAE RENZ
Weaving / 161

SHELLE VANETTEN-LUACES
Eggs / 164

Photos and Bios / 167

Afterword / 187
SHELLE VANETTEN-LUACES

Acknowledgments / 189

Foreword

Young people in America tend to get a bad break these days. Of course that's true of every younger generation. But American teenagers in the early twenty-first century bear a particularly harsh burden. Older folks find their music not only incomprehensible, but often hostile. Professors worry about the future, complaining that freshmen students aren't up to the challenges of a college education. School administrators even try to censor the visibility of underwear in teenage apparel.

While most younger generations are rebellious, twenty-first-century teenagers are made to seem more self-exiled than committed to causes. But readers of this anthology of New Mexican teenage poetry will get a very different and more accurate view of the inner lives of young people living along the cultural fault lines of our state at the turn of the century. *¿de Veras?*, with its passionate, handsomely constructed, openhearted poems, brave and soulful in their candor, is the truth-telling antidote to the stereotypes and slanders of the old against the young.

Each summer from 2002 to 2006, a dozen or more New Mexican teenagers wrote, edited, and performed their poetry for a full month, five days a week, at the National Hispanic Cultural Center (NHCC) in Albuquerque. Building a community among themselves, they collaborated in their own empowerment, guided by poet-mentor Mikaela Jae Renz, NHCC Education Director Shelle VanEtten-Luaces, and visiting poets. The poems they created in this context, one in which they were both trusted and expected to do their best, underscore a central truth of responsible education. Help young people come to the understanding that they are worth their own best efforts, and they will work with devotion to flourish and grow. It's a simple law of the mind. Practice with spirit and persistence and you will progress in the refinement of any skill or ability. Talent is a mysterious blessing that can only be cultivated by practice and the encouragement of energized teachers and eager and compassionate peers.

The writing workshops themselves helped students produce between three to six polished poems by the end of the summer. Combining journal work and other writing practices with structured poetic composition and performance, young poets learned to edit and revise their work and evolve their sense of rigor and standards.

When I read the first of these poems in 2002, all my preconceptions were immediately revised. It seemed to me that these young poets were working up to the height of their talents with remarkable results. The NHCC summer writing program was masterfully conceived and blossoming with gifted students. Mikaela Jae Renz and Shelle VanEtten-Luaces know how to help young people recognize their own potential. They build confidence and encourage communication with useful criticism and comradery, and they do so without the formal and authoritarian hierarchy of regular classrooms. The mentors are part of the community themselves, as shown by the inclusion of their poetry contributions to the annual class-created, handsomely designed, spiral-bound collections of poems. The summer writing program helped to build in these young poets a desire to be not only true and real, but also polished and refined in the sense of becoming demanding workers at their craft.

The result is a collection of revealing, intelligent, and often profoundly emotional poetry, a collection that will take readers into striking new perspectives and new takes on universal themes.

Here's a small part of what's going inside the life of Anthony "WonderBoy" Alaniz, expressed in his poem "My America."

My America simmers—a fantasy locked between these small ears of mine.
The reality is a concrete rain forest where I see broken glass and candy wrappers
    littering the
        streets.
Street cracks leak their way into buildings, decay the structures surrounding
    the glorious Staples Center.
Faceless somebodies walk by faceless nobodies. . . .

Wait, stop.
Take a step back with me and look through the decayed building cracks.
Peer into my mind to see flowers blooming in clear waters. . . .

■

Egla López writes of the universal torments of remorse,

New life
such an innocent soul,
forced to live in this place,

a place where fear, sadness and hate exist.

■

In his poem "Insomniac," Ehren Salazar-Marcrum asks

Do you sleep?
Is it real?
I've listened to you
Twenty-two thousand times before
But I never believed
In your insomnia.

What do you think of
When the sheep stop jumping? . . .

■

In "Invocation," Tamara Bryan reveals a political seriousness that weaves kinship across barriers of age:

We want a revolution
because it's burning on our tongues
and we can taste it like chile
but changing the world is more difficult than
shedding our skin and using it for paper . . .

what we really want
is to use our tongues like a furnace
to reshape the world
because we know our words are hot enough . . .

we can show you a dream with our words
and suddenly you believe

■

Make no mistake, the poets in *¿de Veras?* speak the truth of their lives. They are, indeed, for real.

—V. B. Price, Albuquerque

Preface

Mikaela Jae Renz

As a community planner interested in meaning and place, I look forward to one month of the year especially, when I dedicate myself to building a community of teens and writers at the National Hispanic Cultural Center in Albuquerque, New Mexico.

The poems you find in this book were written by New Mexico teens during the Voces Institute, a month-long creative writing program, between 2002 and 2006. They were inspired outwardly by visiting authors, poets, and artists; the environment of the National Hispanic Cultural Center; the experience of being at the workshop; and tours of the museum exhibitions and permanent art collection. Inwardly, these poems were inspired by the courage of almost seventy New Mexico teens to look at their lives, their neighborhoods, their families, and their cultures in minute and riveting detail and share their amazingly perceptive, sometimes damning, always honest insights.

Something magical happens when respect and creativity swirl together in a room of twenty bright high school students who dedicate themselves to a full month of writing in the spirit of collaboration and deep reflection. Every day is filled with a deeper understanding of the interrelatedness of daily interactions that make us who we are as people, as a culture, as a region, and as a society. For a month, these students with varied experiences, families, and beliefs come together to create a supportive community of writers and questioners.

Every community has its own unique character. Each year, a new group of students enters the Voces program with a commitment to be intensely introspective and intuitive about their own lives and the world around them. During the month, we build a community of respect through conversation and writing. While they have different backgrounds, interests, and talents, they all have a similar commitment to hard work, self-expression, and sharing. This commitment quickly translates into a connection and solidarity that most communities work for years to achieve. As a teacher and more importantly as a member of this group, I am always intensely grateful for the generosity and support students show each other.

Because students are Hispanic, white, black, Native American, and Asian-American, the community we build and the conversations we engage in reflect the larger culture of New Mexico. The voices you hear in the following pages may be teens, but they teach powerful lessons we all need to hear. Like all of us, these students are embroiled in questions about peace and war, race and culture, neighborhoods and community, drugs and addiction, family and love.

The work that you find in this book was created through a process of synthesis born of the students from all over New Mexico—Albuquerque, Española, Santa Fe, Grants, Moriarty, Edgewood, Taos, Roswell, Santa Fe, Las Cruces, Las Vegas, and the Jicarilla Apache Reservation—interacting with each other for seven hours a day, five days a week, for the month of June, at the National Hispanic Cultural Center, with its rich cultural, artistic, and technological resources.

The Voces program is based on the premise that students dramatically improve their writing skills by intensely engaging in the literary arts. The writing mentor and visiting instructors offer guidance as strong, caring, and accomplished role models, encouraging students to interact, improve, and excel. The overall goal is to encourage students to value equally the creative process and the product.

The activities, discussions, reading assignments, art tours, visual journaling, visiting instructors, writing assignments, and presentation workshops are coordinated to provide students with experiences that stimulate creativity and encourage the expression of ideas. Each day includes time to interact, learn, and discuss, balanced by time to reflect, write, and read. Over the course of the month, students write original work, present and discuss it with their peers and instructors, then finally edit, revise, and polish it for oral presentation at the closing ceremony reception for families and friends and for the Voces book, published each year by the NHCC.

Students also received guidance and motivation from visiting instructors with a broad range of style and experience, including published authors and poets, artists, performance poets, and community organizers. Since Voces began, many accomplished writers and artists have participated, including E. A. Mares, Demetria Martínez, Valerie Martinez, Danny Solis, Mike "360" Ipiotis, Lisa Chavez, Maritza Loida Pérez, Levi Romero, Daniel Abraham, Tom Chávez, Mita Saldaña, Linda Piper, Maria Leyba, Juliana Coles, Kenn Rodriguez, Carlos Contreras, Jasmine Sena, Don McIver, Aaron Cuffee, Esther Griego, Elsa Menéndez, Frederico Vigil, Cynthia Cook, Sara Dobel, and Hakim Bellamy.

As a compilation of teen writing, this book provides a small and specific window to the insights of New Mexico youth. The Voces Institute is designed to expose young writers to the different aspects of the world around them, to get them thinking about culture and family, neighborhoods and landscapes, art and architecture, history and current events. These students have a unique perspective on issues all of us wrestle with in our daily lives and as a society.

Students apply to the institute because they are already interested in writing; most already have a voice. The Voces program encourages teens to explore what they already know, question what's given to them as real, and stretch themselves in their writing to express in powerful ways the insights they have to share. Their willingness to take on this challenge is reflected in the range and depth of this collection.

Many of the teens in this compilation are seeped in the expansive culture of spoken word poetry, hip hop, and rap, all strong forms of expression that grow out of, participate in, and push the boundaries of oral tradition. Several of the poems in this collection stem from this redefinition; some fare better on paper than others. They are included here because they offer a reflection of the style and subject matter that communicate to others within this community of teen writers.

The poems chosen for this book show the diversity of perspectives and individuality of voices of New Mexico teens. I was blessed to be present at their creation, and I am honored to share them with you. I hope you learn from them as much as we did from each other. ■

Tamara Bryan

Invocation

We want a revolution
because it's burning on our tongues
and we can taste it like chile
but changing the world is more difficult than
shedding our skin and using it for paper

So we try and make it beautiful
by stringing it together with metaphors
and even the clichés fall
like diamonds from our tongues
and for a moment we feel complete

But what we really want is a revolution
what we really want
is to use our tongues like a furnace
to reshape the world
because we know our words are hot enough

We pray similes will reach your ears like truth
melt them off and then we'll all be open to change
but it's only a fragmented dream until
we can show you a dream with our words
and suddenly you believe ■

2002

Ambrose Vigil

Hard Times

When I'm feeling bad, the shit that people tell me is fake.
As fake as a fairy tale. C'mon give me a break.

That's what I need to tell them sometimes, when they can't help.
I need some space right now; I don't need no wealth.

You got to stay cold inside, that's what I tell myself when I feel alone sometimes.
But I can't cry, I don't tear no more; I love god, so death I don't fear no more.

It hurts when I think back to the day when my uncle left.
I want to fulfill my dreams before I take my last breath.

But when that day comes, say I die before I wake,
All that would be left is a shadow of me or a picture in a frame.

And it makes me feel weird inside, but I know it's the truth.
Some tell me I won't live long; statistics show that's the realistic truth.

But I ain't trying to hear that.
I got enough confidence to take me where I want to go.
And that's how I feel, cause right now that's my main goal.

And I'm gonna do whatever it takes to accomplish it,
And anything that gets in my way, I'ma destroy and move past it. ■

Anisha Imhoff-Kerr

What makes me

I am fifty percent medicine
But five percent sane
When the weather is sunny
My tears fall like rain

I am five percent manic
And five percent depression
But what makes me is
Neither hyperness nor aggression

I am ten percent tired
Two percent mad
Three percent outgoing
Five percent bad

But what makes me myself
Is that last fifteen percent
The part that is all smiles
And happiness that won't relent

Anthony Roybal

I Came . . .

I came from a saddened mother faced with the choice of abortion at eighteen.
I came from a place where no father wanted a place for me in his heart.
    I escaped dream.
I came from a place where a stepfather took father's place to me,
But it wasn't enough; it was just disgrace to me.
I came from a place where you hid your inner self, just to make everyone else happy.
In other words, where I came from was the place I was trying to get away from,
So to make it right for me, the place I couldn't stand is the place I had to stay away from.
The day I can find that inner peace with my insecurity
Is the day when my heart will be curing me, and not fearing me.
Now my getaway is my pen and my pad,
No longer any worries about how it's been with my dad.
When I feel the need, I read,
No more questions about him;
It's just me and the creed. ■

Ashley M. Ellison

Broken Pieces

Angry as a flaming fire, burning out of control.

Feelings more breakable than a pure, thin, wineglass,
Shattered into tiny pieces on the oak wood floor.

Once again I slice my finger,
Dark red blood dripping fast,
As I try to pick up the pieces.

Carlos Contreras

Human Zoo

In a future universe,
the earth spins through whirlwinds
while our children play hopscotch on the octagon playgrounds of turtles' backs.
They hunt for ostriches on the railroads of the past,
on the underground where real records spin and memories last,
where subject matters during compare and contrast,
where ignorance doesn't equal big dicks,
and our children are not baby-sat by Comcast.
Cable does not equal status
and d s l are just three letters of the English alphabet,
but you can bet,
I'll be the alpha-revolutionary
for a world where voices make those that bear them, extraordinary,
Explosive dramatics that blow wind through the mane of lions
and add vibration to that of the roar of kings,
And Puffer Fish Blow Echo Holes Through The Cotton Fields Where
    Freedom Rings . . .
Fuck the gales, Stop the rowing,
Hatred in this abstract universe has been ended.
The pupils of the people have seen the way,
and all barriers have been transcended.
The labyrinth just a playground run on the backs of zebras by children
who realize that black and white DOES NOT MATTER!
Now giraffes run holding hands with necks stretched to see above the horizon;
tangerine tides flow through the hearts of those holding hands with Poseidon.
Zeus will not outshine these electric eels that yield the birth of universe
    and universal,
and Gorillas sift through the mist without rehearsal . . .
For rewards come to those that search beneath the surface

for the stability beneath gilded hearts, and the diversity of
Black hands stroking Yellow arms amidst a Red sunset in the Grayness
    of concrete jungles,
becomes abstract art.
Picasso's brushstrokes could not do justice to the free fall of falcons,
with tips of wings that span numerous years of freedom.
You can paint me a pretty picture,
but you can't make me see it.
I'd rather paint reality with shattered glass and fallen leaves
to isolate the beauty of the jagged edge.
The beauty in the beast,
with exhalation of life at its purest form,
Means of survival in a Human Zoo,
Incarcerated, I-solated,
I wander,
in the midst of the hunted and the hunters,
chain-link cages cripple the wings of doves in mid-flight,
left for the glowing eyes of predators in the night.
War and peace cloud the minds of violent pacifists.
Contradictory beliefs have begun;
the moon may try to outshine the sun to impress the stars . . .

Damien Flores

Asphalt Memories

With the smooth stroke of a pen
they took my land.
My Home.

Little piece of paper
glued to my front door
bright red letters
CONDEMNED.

Destroyed to widen the street.
Oh but we fought
Just like our ancestors Aztec and Apache,
but just like our ancestors, we couldn't defeat
the conquistador.

Conqueror,
whose friends in city hall gave signatures
to help butcher my unappreciated home.
Home,
That witnessed three generations grow
with its terrón brick walls.

Bulldozers came.
Came to destroy.
Oh how we cried as we watched across the street.
We watched our family's history being erased
In clouds of dust
by those
hate-filled machines.

Forever buried in asphalt
are the memories
of holidays and parties,
the smells
of beans and chile,
and the sounds
of children's laughter
and joy.

The devil stands at a podium
declaring his victory among TV news reporters
and campaign supporters.
Wearing a wool suit
and a hard hat instead of the usual Spaniard
armor.

Road officially declared open,
but don't drive east in the right lane.
That's where my bed used to be. ■

EHREN SALAZAR-MARCRUM

Icons

(after Codex Espangliensis, *Enrique Chagoya, 1999, National Hispanic Cultural Center Museum permanent collection)*

No inspiration
Just pretty things
Or sharp things
That make points
And draw blood.
Sins feed on
American minds
And bleed
The life out of
Poor Mickey Mouse
The new American martyr?
Superman died for our sins.
What have you done? ■

Elicia Cardenas

Mi cultura es Mexicana
That's what I am
But people not knowing
Call me anything but what I am
What you don't know is I've been here since 1598
Still, you take my language
My culture, even my land
Expecting me to be like you, cabrón
You think of me
Of what you read
But no, you really don't know my history
So don't think you do
Por soy una Mexicana ■

Jasmine Sena

Crush

I would like not to think of you
To not have you swirl around my brain
For hours on end
To wake up with you there
To go to sleep with you there
And not have you here
It's torture to know I can't have you
It's worse when you smile
If I could only have one hour
I'd open the sky
And invite you on a walk
We could take on an infinite path
That leads to the super unknown
In a parallel space
Oh, I hope to meet you in another lifetime
And have déjà vu of these feelings
I'd turn them into grains of sand
And place them in an hourglass
And when the hour was up
I'd break the glass
Mix the sand with water
Make mud
Then sculpt you and I in a dream
Where the idea of you could be
Surrendered forever ■

Jeremy Maes

(after El Milagro, *1987, shown at an exhibition of Carmen Lomas Garza at the National Hispanic Cultural Center, 2002)*

Three dead rattlesnakes hung,
dripping pools of poisonous blood
on the water tower.
A thousand people had driven
to the middle of nowhere
to see the miraculous image
of the Virgin of Guadalupe.
The crowd was greeted by
a display of death
as the three bullet-ridden
venomous predators
dyed crimson the hem of her dress.
They were a warning,
according to the cowboys who shot them.
They were decked out
in leather boots, jeans and cowboy hats.
The walnut stocks and shiny gray barrels
of their shotguns gleamed in the desert sun.
The warning they gave was in bold red letters,
"Worship here all you want,
but don't go into the cotton field." ■

Kate Twitchell

I am white.
Not albino or Hispanic
          or Chicana
          or black
          or Latina.
Just plain white.
My ancestors are not the ones
who forced yours to change.
Mine have been in search
of religious freedom.
We moved from England
from a family who disowned us
because of our choice of religion.
We moved to join others of our kind.
We fled from other whites
who tortured
     persecuted
     killed us
because they understood
facts about our beliefs
that were not true.
They burned our
beautiful masterpieces
of architecture and
sacrificed our temples
where we had sought
a peaceful abode of worship
in the land where Pilgrims seeking
the same thing
first landed.

We moved West
yearning for a Zion
a promised land
where we could dwell in peace.
We lived in a world
of wagons and bonnets
dust and frostbite
starvation and constant moving
and countless other hardships
that can be described in great detail
because I have lived
through their footsteps
and realized
bit by bit
what they went through
walking blindlessly
to a vision in the objective mind
until we settled
in a valley desert
that no one else wanted
and called it home
    Zion
    Deseret
    Utah
and made it green
Mormon paradise.
I could go on and on
because my heritage
is rich in stories
but the point is
I am white
but I have a heritage too.

KEVIN PACHECO

La Llorona

(after La Llorona, *1989, shown at an exhibition of Carmen Lomas Garza at the National Hispanic Cultural Center, 2002)*

Scared by stories her grandmother used to tell her,
Carmen had a good imagination to go with the story:
La Llorona, the weeping woman
ghost she used to be afraid of,
but now it's just a story she tells in her art.
Across the street from her house was an empty lot filled
with snakes and spiders, and that's where La Llorona
was said to be by her parents.
In Carmen's mind the street was the river,
and she could picture La Llorona
reaching for her children
while they were floating down the street—
the said-to-be river. ■

Khamyra A. Hall

Brown and Proud

Brown and proud
Do you know what that means?
Puro Chicana
No longer will we stand behind the scenes.

A lighter shade of brown
Yes, that's me
But the color of my skin
Isn't all you can see:

See the brown
Is the color of the land I'm from
The land that we worked as
We browned in the sun.
See the brown
The color of our blood
Dried and stained
On the history of my people
Who are done wrong to this day.
See the brown
That colors my "angel eyes"
My long brown hair
That could touch my soft thighs.
See the brown
That I am so proud to be
The color of la raza
Mi gente . . . of me

Our culture is . . .
Lowriders on Friday nights
Music bumping in the systems
Barrios lit by luminaria light
La posadas
Y fiestas to show.
Our culture is familia.
I just wanted to let you know.

I am brown and proud
And I am going to take the stand.
As my ancestors before me
For my people
For my land
To show we are proud to be brown.
Chicana is who I am. ■

Marcelo Moya

Preparation for the Future

The beautiful sound of jackhammers and big giants backing up, beautiful sound of something breaking. The wonderful smell of dark air polluting your lungs, the smell of dust, of history, all being blown away. The best feeling of power, of choosing for others, of making someone cry. The best way to take someone is to take their culture and replace it with a machine. Nothing gets better than making the neighborhood turn into a plant for mothers to raise their kids to be shipped to jail so that we can say they need our help. We are freeing people from the binds of their homes and hope. If only the world lost all hope then we could say, how lovely is the world today?

Marisol Servizio and Khamyra A. Hall

Imprisonment

Too many bars
too many walls
holding me down and in.
Have you noticed that it seems only one person,
one voice keeps getting shut up in the prisons?
Are they afraid of what we do?
Or are they afraid of what we could?
It is only so long before the oppressed become oppressors,
but they don't realize that we were meant for so much more.
Graffiti is a crime?
Well, where do we paint our stories
about how we spend our lives in the hood
or inside your cages killing time?
We come out after too long
and no longer know how to fly,
forced into a celled world that is not our reality
to find too much of life has passed us by,
too many opportunities gone,
too many lonely friends and families left to cry.
This is what is done to our future,
locked up and silenced away.
Once all of us are gone,
who will be left to build your brighter day?

A brighter day, unknown to you—
time taken away.
Now you control my life time,
changing days to years.
Big hand of my days
controls hours I've slowly lost,
small hand of years,
wasted in the cage you contain me in.
Crime is anything you see me do—
the expression of my pride
that bursts from colored cans of my heart.
See the picture I draw?
Clowns in this cage,
laughing at what lies inside.
The tip of my pen
creates the picture of my life. ■

MATTHEW LUCERO

True Wealth

True wealth is not what I had always thought.
True wealth is not something you have bought.
It's about what you've been taught.
I know what you have sought—
A car, guitar, getting drunk at the bar.
We shouldn't have to go that far.
Play a game of golf and get a par,
Don't try to make up for it by buying a car.
True wealth is not smoking pot and letting your soul rot.
TV tries to treat you like a robot.
It tells you to buy more till you drop to the floor.
Do it and your body becomes sour.
You buy one and you're ready to buy four.
Now it's time to implore about your fake reality.
Can't you see everything you buy has a fee?
Money doesn't grow on trees. ■

Rebecca Ortega

Denim Jeans: An American Icon

Invented by Levi Strauss in 1872,
Stone-washed, denim, black,
White, low-rise, cargo,
Capris, and shorts—
Any types you can imagine.

Capris can push the pedals to the limit.
Cargo pants are the best,
Because they have pockets to hold
Enough bullets for the fight against pleather,
Yet leather is the protection against the battle. ■

Samantha Emord

The Tower

I stand before a tower of fresco; empty white walls stare at me from every direction.
They are the unfinished walls of the *Torreón*, the tower.
One man creates this masterpiece. Alone.
I gaze helplessly at the vast height of the circular tower encasing me.
I could never be capable of such a feat as the one this man has accomplished.
That's what I've told myself all these years, and now I've finally begun to believe it.
Vivid colors pasted to the wall give a small bit of life to its emptiness.
Bright, colorful lines try, one step at a time,
To bridge the crevasse between my mind and theirs.
But my mind is trapped,
Trapped in a place where the walls are thicker
Than the imagination can dream them,
A place where all doors are locked and bolted not with a key,
But with something much stronger: the mind.
But these are not the minds of humans;
They are the minds of powerful creatures that
Enslave the weak-minded.
They wreak havoc on the poor beings who are not fortunate
To have the abilities to overpower their torturers.
I try to forget my situation
By staring intently at the beautiful creatures on the walls.
They are so free.
They have no real shape, no real being,
For now, at least.
Soon they will be free enough to fly out into the imagination,
And from there, anywhere.
I am so much like them: I don't know my purpose or what MY actual being is.
If unreal creatures can create themselves into being
And break all boundaries enclosing them, then nothing is impossible.
And with that, my mind escapes. ■

Sara Humphreys

Revelation

She stands there all alone
Her voice drowning time
She takes hold of the world
And you cannot tell whether
She is guiding the chaos
Or calling forth the calm. ■

Mikaela Jae Renz

El Té, Alfredo Ceibal, 1986

The flatness of the floor
was the one-sided view of Columbus
sailing off the edge of the world

Your four walls caging you in
the flimsy clay already melting
in the mestizo sun

Your indio feathers
couldn't fan the flames of your words
stop them from igniting revolution
as the town tipped downward
wiping itself clean
and starting again
to rise like Phoenix from barren earth

Your party drunkenness
should have been your hint
that everything tips
everyone's tipsy-turvey
and turning worlds
turn blank slates
into civilization
with golden kings on pyramid tops
and burnt-red slaves on the bottom

(the big fat bottom of lazy wives
pulling decorated husbands
obsequiously behind enormous behinds)

What is behind your flat-floored ballroom
what money what power what chains
shore up your wet clay-pot walls
twisting and curving and tearing apart?

Tearing down and building up
new generations of dictators
who sit laughing
drunk with power and native-made brew
while polite neat servants
serve up civility and obedience
that will keep you awake tonight
with indigestion
that slowly kills them faster
than the hard manual labor
that built you this house of falling stones ■

Shelle VanEtten-Luaces

The Problem with Males and Art

hiding in the bathroom, quietly behind the door. . . .
flipping through my journal of unfinished sketches and half-captured insights
agonizing over incomplete pieces, abandoned visions—
i identify two problems.

one: my artistic life blossoms when i am unattached to a male
two: i have spent fourteen weeks of my adult life unattached to a male

slipping into a vision of life as an artist,
living a quiet existence of incredible success, filled with beautiful finished
pieces adorning my walls, their walls, gallery walls. . . .

then,

pushing and pounding on the bathroom door . . .
"mommy, mommy . . . where you are. . . .
mommy, mommy . . . where you—
there you are!"

falling onto my lap, my one-year-old knocks my journal to the floor—
squealing to find me hiding as if waiting for peek-a-boo,
throwing his arms around my neck, my two-year-old whispers "uh-oh"
as my pen rolls behind the toilet
taking with it another almost-captured idea
and i identify two overwhelming truths.

one: i will never be unattached to a male again
two: i have created and completed two works of art in my adult life,

and they are both male ■

2003

Ambrose Vigil

Shadows of Death and Last Breaths

Look in my eyes; take a journey in my mind.
Shadows of death and last breaths are a different kind
Than you would've imagined.
What you see is something unique
The physical form of someone you haven't
Seen before, someone you deplore.
Devastating scenes, no hesitation—strictly force,
Pointed directly at your presence.
Now you're in a position where you don't understand your essence,
So you don't test this
Unknown figure.
Drug dealers, thugs, and killers are people you may fear,
But they're not even equal to the tears of those you have witnessed.
It's impossible to be optimistic,
But it's more than possible to be twisted on the pavement
With an engraving on the left side of your chest
Of a casket representing your death.
No stabbings or shootings, they don't exist.
This new breed of last breaths is something you would dream to miss.
Fiend and wish for better days.
Even if you're blessed with a gift you have still felt pain,
Rage burning in your soul.
Your taste buds crave an eternal insane way of the old.
Your mind is stuck in the past.
With one life to live, you might as well make it last. ■

Anisha Imhoff-Kerr

That Person Is Me

I am a person
Look at me
Ten fingers, ten toes
Regular hair
Maybe a little ruined by dye
Perhaps shorter than you in height
I am ten times taller than you in knowledge
I am younger
But wiser
Why?

I have been to hell and back
Don't think about my journey
You'll never understand
Just look at me
Look at my face
Two eyes, a mouth, a nose
I look like you
I look normal
I look like myself

What's inside my head
That is what matters
Believe it or not, there is a brain
It can do calculus
It can write
A brain that is bipolar

Yes I look like you
But our similarities end there!
Our brains set us apart
Mine is a gift

I can stay up all night for days at a time
Accomplish things bigger and better than required
Live in a mental state
Where all is happy
Where the energy is high
The whole world seems to be running slower than I am
Words like "grandiosity," "high-strung," and "fast-paced"
Pop out of psychiatrists' mouths
Then "wild," "out of control," and "a danger to herself"

The times when the world seems empty
I stay in bed for weeks at a time
There is no hope
The world, however, is not crashing down on everyone's head
There is no need for a Chicken Little here
The only world falling is mine
Consumed by my dark thoughts
I could disappear and the rest of the world wouldn't even know it

To stop myself from spinning out of control
I have to work
I have to work and suffer so I can be like you
My journey through hell
Not the hell with pits of fire
No orange flames licking at my toes

Modern medicine:
Drugs to make you normal
Balanced
Like the rest of the world
Drugs that cause your hair to fall out
Your skin to peel off
Your vision changes every three days but hey
You got a 45 percent discount at the optometrist
Your thinking capacity is diminished
Your stomach won't accept any food
Lamictal, Topamax, Neurontin, Tegretol, Trileptal, Zonisamide, Depakote
I've tried them all
And in between every one of these "new and improved," "medically tested" drugs
Medicine was always brought back to the oldest,
Most trusted
"Wonder drug" called Lithium
It helps manic depression, but makes people sicker than dogs

All I ever wanted was a normal, balanced life
But like everything in life
There was a price
And I paid
With my loss of faith
With desperation
With people losing faith in me
I lost friends
Family members grew distant
I visit the ER every other month

I miss half the school year, every year
I am sick every day
And for what?
So I can be like you?
Because you won't accept me if I'm not like you

Worst of all
Before I was diagnosed
Before they told me I was "Bipolar One Mixed with Psychosis"
I was the happiest I had ever been
Because I was happy being me ■

Ashley M. Ellison

for Victor Gonzalez

I was partially insane from all the drugs I took
But instead of turning away, you gave me
Another look.

You asked me,
"Why do you seem to be in so much pain and misery?
Why do you do so many drugs?
And why do you waste your life hanging with thugs?
You could rise above all of this."

What happened next was like a game of chance.
Love bound us together when life was hard.
At times we lost each other,
But the dealer had already dealt us our cards,
Stuck together like the King and Queen of hearts.

I still can't see very far down the road
Or what turns could be up ahead.
But at least I have those turns to anticipate—
If it wasn't for you, I would already be dead.

You helped me get where I am and set my soul free,
You showed me happiness and what my life could be.

A life not yet lived would have been tragic. ■

Carlos Anderson

Silence is sometimes the best answer
And there are times to speak out
But you have the right to remain silent
Or the cops will tweak out.
Miranda rights—that's what mag lights are good for.
The other day a diabetic was nearly beat to death for being impatient—
Impatient that he was going to die without his insulin.

You see, real police don't need a gun, just a stick of gum.
At times people just need to talk to someone.
The other day a brotha was pulled over
And the backup unit thought his cell phone was a potential lethal weapon.
Six rounds spent.
I hope he went to heaven.
Is that justice?
No.
If it was, then society must list
All the wrongs of the righteous
Just as lifeless as the people they killed
Just for that shrine they build to commemorate
The death of interracial hate.

But I've seen what justice can't.
She's blind, but she sees right through me.
Like a movie the plot is resolved.
Eventually we are
The problem and the answer.
We are neither
Of the cancer. ■

Carlos Contreras

You
White wings of alabaster
Thieving parts of heart
As I examine the curvatures of your face
With inside of palm to cheekbone
Enjoying brown on white skin tone
Like White Sands
Meets Chaco Canyon

She sheds light on the existence of
Broken-English
And
Tangled-tongue Spanish but
Words from a pair of lips have never seemed so perfect
Perhaps that's what I fear most
That I'll believe her
For I no longer possess forked tongue to deceive her
Just hearts where my sleeves were

You see
I'm wandering now
Naked lost and cold
In a world so
Big brash and bold
That I hope I don't
Stumble crash or fold

But just in case
I've begun discreetly chopping up and
Folding pieces of my heart
Placing them in places
Where they will be void of discovery

Beneath my tongue
Under my bed
Behind the whites of my eyes
Acting as
Subconscious
Self-conscious
Venetian blinds
Bringing new meaning to the old saying about
"Eyes being windows to the soul"

but for you'd I'd roll
thumb to forefinger
thumb to forefinger
thumb to forefinger
and draw the sun in for you

I want to wrap you in blankets of breath
And bathe you in
Forget-me-not kisses

I want to unfold your heart
And delicately crease myself
Back in-between your most forgotten beats
So that we can make music together
Something funky like
OutKast meets Garth Brooks
And we'll have tone-deaf angels and
Satan's armies
Singing hooks because
Nobody's perfect

Though we'd like to be
I'd like to be for the simple fact that you're liking me
Your capability of code-switching entices me
You've become the stage that brings out the mic in me
Now let's perform ■

Demi Olivas

Beauty to Pieces

300,000 km/sec
Life rays reflecting off me
Displaying colors of blue purple and gold

Colors that dance leap twirl
And spread wings
Like the lifeless beauty butterfly
Flapping and expanding
Swaying like the lone limb.

They create a gust
An enormous whirlwind.
It carries me off on the rim of its pull

Violent drafts of gentle jolt
Crude acts of loving assault

To a place where
The lion lies with the lamb
A drowsy infant rests upon the alligator's tongue
Man loves man.

Here flowers do not wilt
Trees forever remain green
And when gravity pulls them down
They transform into muses.
Who speaks such loving words of inspiration?

Wake up!
You're still sleeping.
You see this place does not exist
A figment of my mind
A photon of my light
A particle too small to be seen.

Allow me to enlighten you.

Society:
Ritual mannerisms maintained
Programmed
Like mechanically engineered dolls
Hypnotic
Such puppets to our master's strings
And
All audibility is purely subliminal
Tongues.
Let's paint our faces
And
Parade around the town.

But underneath this makeup emerges a hidden cave of
shadows
Securing
Black lies
Fake cries
Discreet deceit.

One so bold would not dare enter
For this dragon cannot be slain.

With bloodstained hands
We
Possess no conviction
Only unnecessary gestures
Non-required greetings
An illusion of purity
A mirage of good intentions.
Self-benefit is the only value.

We
Deny our faults
Dismiss all charges.

Hypocrite.
Who me?
Yes you.

Forgive me, I was volunteered
I was engineered
Manufactured by the world

No wave of hope.

Religion:
Dear priest,
Black out my eyes
Adorn them with staples

Deny me
Defy me
Transform me into you.
Tattoo my skin with permanent ink
Cut out my memory
Erase all of my dreams
Oh gut out my soul
Place it in your piggy bank

Covet my identity
My skin to a quilt
Then
Cover yourself in it
And
Let it shroud all of your sins.

Scapegoat
Scapegoat
Preacher
Preacher
My priest please
Be my teacher.

Molest the new infant baptized
Consume the red rich wine
Lie to the people and deny them their time.

But I know your secret.
It creeps over the horizon
Bright lights of red orange and yellow
Overt with each light particle.

Soon the quilt will begin to unravel.
Holes will be punched through.
A light of darkness will shine.
It's going to illuminate the room.

Scapegoat
Scapegoat
Preacher
Preacher
No one knows
But he still sees ya.

Get with the fucking program.
Manipulation makers
Monastery fakers
And yes I'm talking to you.

Shh . . .
Can you hear that?
It's the gurgling sounds of my oppressed brothers
Muffled by the pillow nights American dream
Choked by the media's deceit
Crushed by the palm of my fellow dictators
You and me.

Take some responsibility.
My brothers
My sisters

We are all bound by the same spirit
Spawn in the womb of the same creator.

She birthed us
Then left
Remains
Doesn't matter.

You see
When that whirlwind carried me off on the rim of its pull
I did not land in fairyland.
I didn't even leave home

A place where the lion consumes the lamb
The alligator feigns for carnivorous meat
Man hates man.

Here petalled flowers droop.
Trees age with my guilt.
Leaves fall off of trees
Flowing with the wind
Deteriorating
Gone.

You picked all the leaves from the trees that fall.
We picked all the leaves from the trees that fall.
I picked all the leaves from the trees that fall.

Oh but when they fell,
Muselike figurines,
They did inspire. ■

EGLA LÓPEZ

Remorse

New life
such an innocent soul,
forced to live in this place,

a place where fear, sadness and hate exist,
where people care more about material items than anything else,

where money speaks, where corruption rules,
but what people don't realize is that it will come back to them,

maybe not in this lifetime but the next,
a place where they will have time to realize their mistakes,
but by then it will be too late.

Ehren Salazar-Marcrum

Insomniac

Do you sleep?
Is it real?
I've listened to you
Twenty-two thousand times before
But I never believed
In your insomnia.

What do you think of
When the sheep stop jumping?
They only stare at you
With that stupid gaze
Only farm animals
Can give.
I find it
Terrifying.

Do you stalk about your empty house
Like a large white cat
Scratching the furniture
And pissing on the walls?
Or do you fill your house
With light
Artificial of course
Pretending it's the sun?
That would be fitting.

Do you watch television
Blue images of anthropomorphic
Caricatures blowing each other to bits
Wondering why
You are awake
And alone?

Felicia Herrera

She said she wanted to leave the country and explore the sky

Have ten children but not in this lifetime
Drop in the middle of the ocean and not drown

She said she wanted to walk into the fires of hell but not feel the heat

Get into people's minds even if she hasn't met them
Change the world with her voice and not be hated

She said she wanted to fall asleep next to her lover even though she didn't have one

Keep her mother under her grave
And hug her to bring her back to life

She said she wanted to be released from the world but thinks life can only get better

Graciela Gonzales

New Mexico

My mother plants lavender wherever she steps.
The scent mixed in with Spanish broom,
the infamous smell of sage,
makes Sandia Mountains red.
Golden yellows and blood reds paint the sky so
only a little blue can seep through at the top of the canvas.
Dry heat makes clothes skimpy and skin golden tan.
Only New Mexico can do this.
Water is scarce,
But one can always smell the rain before it falls.
When it does it is like a prayer from god,
the way it fills and seeps into my body.
Horses run and gallop until their
pintos, blacks, and browns blend into one.
The Rio Grande twists and turns like veins in my body,
and I know that I can always find my reflection among its waters.
New Mexico has an abundance of red rock
and even more, clay.
But New Mexico
is New Mexico
is Nuevo Mexico,
and it is my home.

Jasmine Sena

Soak up a sudden or violent
Gust of wind
Sound or force
Of some kind
Incline toward each other
A sweet preparation
Something made up
To figure out the
Meaning of uncertain outcomes
I saw her mix her coffee
With her finger
And I could tell she was
Thinking something crazy
She had the look of
A woman trying to find out
How far the elastic in her
Panties can stretch
And that morning she
Spent most of her time trying
To find lost meaning of life in
Early recorded Jimi Hendrix tracks
The bitch in her voice
Told me she felt
A little more enlightened
She never noticed the
Blinding glare she gives off
Thinking all car accidents are
Meant to be
And the other day she
Fell out of love with herself
She felt it was time
To move on
And time
She didn't even know what
Day it was
But it didn't matter 'cause

The sun was about to set
And soon night would take over
It always seemed more
Calm in the dark
She lit a cigarette
And puffed away her demons
Came back
And tried to loosen her
Tight thoughts on how
She feels uneasy
When she thinks about the
Thought of just being
And some days
About 12:15
Dreams seemed like
They had no meaning
Far away where they
Can't be seen
In between
Word schemes
And silent music
You could see her
Wear and tear
She's fighting the feeling
To pull her hair
Slash her arm
Bite her nails
Move on
Move on
Keep on keeping on
And on
And on
Keep on keeping on
And on
And on
'Til she STOPS ■

Jeremy Maes

Isms

I'm against Catholicism
I don't mean to offend Catholics when I say this
It's just that Catholicism is an ism
And I don't believe in isms
Isms in my opinion are a dangerous thing

I mean look at all the isms that are in the world today:
Socialism
Capitalism
Literalism
Criticism
Sadism
Sexism
Harry Potter-ism
Running your husband over three times with a Buick-ism
Alcoholism
Mormonism
Cthulhuism

Raneejhism
Chaoism
Taoism
Maoism
Buddhism
Satanism
Racism
Marxism
Fascism
Terrorism
And worst of all, feminism

I don't believe in isms
I quote John Lennon
"I don't believe in Beatles, I just believe in me."
That's a good philosophy
But if I can only believe in myself
I'd rather be an atheist. ■

Misused Toys

She sat in her room playing with the plastic pony. Her next-door neighbor had snapped off its leg and given it to her when it didn't seem beautiful anymore. She accepted it with open arms, played with it alongside her other toys, and understood that even though it was broken, it could stand strong if it was leaned up against something stable.

A knock came from her window and echoed through her room. Using all the strength her five-year-old muscles could manage, she pushed her plastic box of toys underneath the windowsill and climbed victoriously on top.

A man stood below her window and signaled for her to come to him. Without hesitation she jumped from her box, stumbled out of her room, and exited her back door. She ran straight into the stranger's arms. He put her down and gestured for her to follow him.

He headed for the woods behind her backyard, and she followed playfully. He turned around and reached for her clumsily. She pulled away in fear, but he soothed her fast-beating heart with a "shh." His shaking hands undressed her frail body until she was left naked in the sun streaming through the trees above. He laid her down, and as the dried pine needles dug into her baby-soft back, he caressed her trembling body with callused fingers. He dragged his heavy tongue across her canvas of childhood and dug inside her with his penetrating stare. She whimpered.

He picked her up so he could watch her struggle to get dressed. She walked away, left herself behind, doing her best to kiss her innocence good-bye. The man she didn't know stole it, and she was left, in shame, to deny ever leaving the safety of home.

Back in her room, she reached for something, or someone, to lean on. Finding no one, she collapsed beneath her beauty. ■

Nikki Poindexter

The Land of Enchantment

New Mexico . . . land of enchantment!
BAH!
If I were to sum it up into one phrase,
the phrase would be very similar to:
godforsaken wasteland!
I mean, what do people see out here?
There are approximately
two
oxygen molecules per cubic foot
and even less water than that!
The local "trees" are no more
than shrubbery on steroids
and
everything
is
BROWN!
The water is
BROWN!
The sky is
BROWN!
Even the dead grass is
BROWN!
There's hardly anything green at all,
and you couldn't
hide in what passes for a forest around here
to save your life!
The "rainstorms" last about
.2 seconds before evaporating into the dusty sky.

And the god-awful stench of wet
earth! It smells utterly foul, like something just
died!
Give me real *trees* dammit!
GREEN TREES!
I want to see the ocean again,
even if it is clogged in a perpetual twilight
due to the vast, thick covering of gray clouds
blanketing the sky for weeks on end,
leaving everyone west of the Cascade Mountains albino
and fearing the sun like Erik the Viking
I still miss it!
But NO! Ooooh no! I'm
stuck *here*!
In a landlocked, dead-colored, dust-coated,
moisture and vegetation deprived wasteland!
Yeah . . . the land of enchantment alright . . .
for the UNDEAD! ■

Penny Chimal

When Elk Hooves Chatter

Wind blows, leaves rustle
Starry sky, smoky clouds
Your feet moving side to side
Your arms held up high

Flames burn
The smell of hichede
Fills the air
Silent prayers all around
There are no other sounds

Images of your lifetime
Slowly come, slowly go
White painted woman
You become in the morning

Gramma grass brushing against your skin
Everything painted white
With the exception of your buckskin

Then you run
It's not like the first morning
Where you run coming in
The farther you go
The more you have from within

All the hope in your heart floats
Smiles upon you
Hugs around you
You have earned your name and
All the blessings that surround you ■

Revé Chewiwi

La Chola

I remember the sting
Of a fist on my face
One regretful thing
Blocked my eyes like space
The recollection still sounds
Of a young chola life
The way I was down
Always packing a knife
I still hear the cheers
The whistles and cries
The scent of beers
And ongoing lies
I remember a life
That many dare not live
A heart full of strife
I no longer want to live
But I remember the day
I fell on my knees
And began to pray
God help me please
I remember the joy
That welled up in my soul
No longer Satan's toy but to heaven I'll go

Samantha Emord

Writing Pains

She said it's because
She doesn't understand.

She doesn't understand
How the words can
Flow so easily from her tongue
But stick in her fingers
Like cold molasses.

She doesn't understand
Why words seem out to get her.
The wrong ones come out at all
The wrong times
And the right ones stay
In her mouth
Caged
Like Brazilian macaws.

She'd like to find refuge
In writing
But the truth is
The thought of blank paper
Terrifies her.
It embodies all her presentiments
Of being powerless
To fix things.
She knows not everyone
Can do everything
But if it weren't for
Her lack of foresight
Her inability to say the
Right things
Things might be different.

You see
16th of December rolls around and
People aren't cheering for Christmas.
They're crying for
The death of a boy
Who she knows
She could have helped
Could have said something more.
Paid more attention.
Maybe then he wouldn't
Have striven for attention on the
Backs of moving cars.

But she knows
That her regrets
Would have done nothing
But take her pain away.
She knows that death
Is unconquerable
And because fields of snow
Symbolize death
She thinks a white piece of paper
Is too much for her to handle.

For now she just wants to
Change the color of paper
From white snow to blue skies
And maybe then
The molasses in her fingers
Will melt to water
And the pain will melt away. ■

Samantha Innis

He Was, She Was, They Were

He was like a catapult
Shooting fake emotions through her heart.
She was like a shooting star
Shooting for
Someone to love
And missing every time.
The sky was like a tower
Shadowing her world.
The Earth was like magnetic sin
Attracting her to him. ■

Mikaela Jae Renz

Connect the dots
Injustice
  to
      Injustice

Cultivate the will
   the fortitude
   the stomach
to call shit as you see it
                  name it
                  change it
                  arrange it

Complicit in the world-as-it-is
   is our silence

We trade "solace" for "privacy"
   "community" for "solitude"

We hide our gifts
    not to feel powerless
  close our eyes
     not to feel blind
  believe stories
     not to feel lied to

Our ears wither
     with disuse
Our fears grow
   with exercise
Our hands
    severed with knives of our own creation
    search by themselves for the necks of our oppressors
And we
    all of us children
    learn what it is
    we don't want to know

Shelle VanEtten-Luaces

I'm Two

"I'm two."
Yes, you're two chubby, sand-covered, energetic feet
engaging in feats of balance and adventure
that leave my heart both
pounding at potential disaster and beaming at your bravery

"I'm two."
Yes, you're two sumo-strength, Energizer-Bunny legs—
a leg up on the chair, the table, the kitchen counter,
climbing towards that bag of chocolate—
that I watch running full speed towards your life

"I'm two."
Yes, you're two scraped up, scratched up, dusty knees—
kneeling down to look eye to eye with a snail or to push a truck—
that I cover daily in Band-Aids, antiseptic and kisses

"I'm two."
Yes, you're two strong, sweaty sticky, brown hands
handing me found treasures of rocks, cut paper, strange sticks
that I accept enthusiastically with great affection

"I'm two."
Yes, you're two golden open arms
armed with a ball, a book, a big blue marker,
a bottle of warm milk at the end of the day,
which is the time when all you want is to be in my arms

"I'm two."
Yes, you're two young, healthy, strong lungs
laughing, screaming, crying, laughing, singing,
which breathe in the wonder of the world,
breathe out sweet baby breath

"I'm two."
Yes, you're two perfectly open ears
listening to my songs,
which I sing in the quiet of the night and early mornings

"I'm two."
Yes, you're two perfectly shaped, Popsicle-flavored lips—
lips on cheek, on my other cheek—
that whisper nonsensical secrets into my ear and my heart

"I'm two," my baby says.
Yes, you're two bright hopeful eyes,
which I want to shield from everything that will
turn your bravery to fear,
slow your legs,
make you hide your treasures,
pull you from my arms,
silence your voice,
quiet your listening,
and steal your secrets and kisses. ■

2004

Ambrose Vigil

For the Love of Hip Hop

i brand my thoughts with realness
lace and trace my elements with illness
feel this internal passion
part-time verbal assassin
label me a nocturnal beast that creeps when you sleep
while you hope to continue
to proceed with your dreams
or so it seems
you're blind at night when it's the darkest
gimme a mic so i can spark this
cause that's when i play
my words rotate like they have a boundary gate
spherical shaped
creatin' lyrical miracles to expose to those that hate
i'm quick to retaliate and leave the scene with nothing but ashes and dust
i slice and dice like a guillotine every time i bust
i don't give a fuck what the next man does cause
in hip hop i trust
i must activate what's real cause i don't follow and do everything the same
don't hate the playa hate the game
don't hate the poet hate the stage
for bringing out my presence
it's my essence to liquefy what i write and show my vigorous side
cats try to get rigorous on the mic when they rhyme
but that shit is obsolete
they need to take time to think before they speak
cause years ago was when that got old
but it don't really bother me cause real hip hop is still the nucleus of my soul
the flesh of my flesh

because of that I have witnessed the mystic depths beyond depths
i've been victimized by the rhythm of lyrics
this is only the root of my voice that you're hearing
and people still get shook
i'm like a disconnected phone cause i'm off the hook
i take a look at the past, the way i act
react to facts, slash cash
mash and smash on the ones that think i won't last
i don't understand why i'm looked at as an outkast
instead of it being me
why not see the ones that are only in it for the money and fame
running deep within their veins
this shit is like a lethal injection to 'em
and they're still trying to shoot it in their blood
trying to be a flowatician, vokalist, poet, or an emcee
what about me
i'm all of the above
with a prophetic state of mind
something you might label mighty fine
the only time you will see me with krylon is when i'm displayin' my name on cloud 99
it's pointless to try to pull me down
cause ain't no man alive that can darken my shine ■

BRITTANY JEWEL

Puppet Strings

The puppet strings yank and pull
Making her walk, making her dance
She weeps, for she's captive

They say the story played out well
The sky refused to tell
The trees stood witness
The ground told her secrets

One summer day she cut her strings
Opened her arms, breathed in the break of dawn
We awoke one day to find she was gone ■

Chasity A. Vigil

Intolerance

Have you ever seen the evils of life—
of the earth and the people?
Have you ever seen a person get beaten
or seen someone destroy a life—
watch their family cry?
Have you ever seen a child all alone in a corner
because of a so-called color?

Our history speaks of this—
of the evils of the holocaust
slavery and segregation—
the racism that never ends.

How do you classify people?
By their color or race
or how they talk or where they're from
or maybe their religion?

To me all human beings are clear.
They are no color at all.
They all speak a language—
not one in specific,
and they all live on land—
it does not matter where.

So tell me if these are the truths I have spoken
that are oblivious to the world.
Then why did I know it—
a girl fifteen years old—
and why not a scholar, the pope or a king,
who supposedly know everything?

Maybe because I watch and listen and pay attention
to what people say and do
and set myself apart
with my own thoughts and my own views.

People will always be people—
nothing less, nothing more,
and that is how it should be.
Maybe that is how it could be.

Demi Olivas

Vanity

I am coyote.
long ago
I met water on the shores of eternity.
nightly, when the moon
showed itself in water's face,
we'd visit, water and I.
I taught him to love me.
as the moon grew more ancient
against water's surface
my love told me the secrets
of future wars
and chaos theory.

I am coyote who does
not reflect like the moon.
I taught the water to love me.
I am the chaos theory
of future wars.

my jealousy drew water into my throat
and pissed him onto the surface
of a wooden frame.
I poured in clipped
wings, eagle feathers
mixed with clotted horse blood,
tossed in long narrow bodies of
ancient goddesses, perfume, and
rain clouds that will
never fall.

I mixed in the false hope of
water's love for me.

lastly, I took death from
the hollow of my eyes
and spat on the surface.
I carried the tainted water to
the porch of a carpenter
who hung it on his wall,
called it mirror.

the carpenter gazes
into it and does not
understand the secret
of future war.
his hands mimic many.
he will give
them as gifts to
women, men,
children.

as the moon grows more ancient
against my howl I remember
the cancer I poured in,
the death I took from the hollow
of my eyes.
I smile
to the intangible
future war.
it has already begun.

Graciela Gonzales

Emotions that Come with Death and War

(response to a print by Carlos Cortez)

a box comes home warm
red white and blue
cloth keeping in Middle East heat

the family knows that sand
not dirt
is still
under the fingernails

they are not soldiers
but soil-ders
because American soil is sacred
and they chose to protect the grains

if it was their freedom of choice
then why do I feel I should be with the family
in print?

maybe because bodies kept warm
by star spangled banners
make me feel cold

like the families

maybe because I recognize
the grains of sand
under their nails as
the same soil I stand on

it only takes images like these
for me to understand
the newscasters' numerical death reports
on the morning news

this print is from the 1960s
but we're not in that century anymore
and pictures of red white and blue covered coffins
are no longer
in print ■

Gregorio Garcia

Creation

a shallow stream of azure aqua slowly slithers
along the ridged amethyst mountain peaks
remnants of sea life embedded into the floor
ancient trees wiry stand tall
lusciously full of life
pine needles, pinecones blanket
the surface of the earth
childhood memories race beyond comprehension
thoughts of sorrow overpower the good
as the good is lost into the mix
the past ever fading away into the sunset
the future is only now being created
with each passing second all our dreams and childhood fantasies constructed
untold stories of triumph and faith cloud the air
blurring the vision
although nothing is for certain
we all have a future
moving through life all together
not as one but as many
for life is meaningless
without others

Isaiah Baca

Monja Coronada

It's pitch black
Worries in my head
Chills down my back

My spine shivering
My body's quivering

I can't see my hands
I can't see past my pupils
I'm turning in circles
Holding my breath while my face turns purple

I can't see my moves
I know I'm gonna lose
Cause my soul is one big bruise

I'm set out on a mission
But I don't know what it is
I don't know what I'm missin'
I don't have a clue

My life is a twisted cuento
Please help me find my mission
Cause I can't make a decision without
Understanding this twisted mission ■

Jasmine Sena

Paper napkins are no place
for thoughts or feelings
Neither are
sleeves or dreams

and only sand can slide through
the hourglass

I'm still a little naïve about the world
about love
about life

Growing is an itch in the middle of my foot
that I can't scratch because it tickles

My heart is the fist in my throat
that makes it hard to swallow
At the end of nightmares
I can't seem to scream

Right at dawn
life becomes a tedious path to follow

A hit to the head
a loss of consciousness
finding infinity behind my eyes was an awakening
and I've realized nothing

All the colors of all the rainbows
can't comfort me

I'm learning what it is to be a woman

I have all these things going on
so many of them are left in the air
it's become a point to write
to clear them
and all wrong intentions

not quite like confessing
and I'd die before I said I was exhaling

There's a point where gravity
no longer has a hold of you
and now
I'm heavier than the whole world

I feel maybe I've been here before
but the trees are different
and the nighttime beat of lullabies
has left my feet

It's funny that I would find myself
in such places
squares of gray

and I've noticed
night and day
are just different shades of blue

I'm beautiful
true realization ■

JENNIFER OTERO

Where I Come From

I come from the busy streets of an unknown land.
Surrounded by a crowd of people
I feel so lost.
I remain unnoticed.
I linger around
unheard.

I crave being noticed.
I yearn to be heard
yet I'm one insignificant voice
among
HUGE
HUGE
voices.

In time
I will be a voice for my people—
an advocate for the chicanos of America—
no longer lost in the crowd
known
everywhere
as a
hero. ■

Kaly Thayer

Three Guys in My Neighborhood

Where were you when three guys in my neighborhood didn't come home that night?
Where were you when smoke wound up on my horizon?
What happened to the land of the free
thinking?
and the home of the brave
people?
You wave your red white and blues
but will you defend them?

Carbon monoxide chokes me.
My eyes water with smoke and unshed tears.
My neighbor's dad
a friend who took me sailing
a guy who threw great barbecues—
three guys who
didn't come home that night.

Al-Qaeda: they aren't religious zealots
no
they don't deserve the label
that denotes a system of faith.
Their only rule: he who kills the most wins.

Who pays the price
of their blood sacrifice?
Three guys in my neighborhood didn't come home that night
the night bin Laden dialed 9-1-1
an international call
made in American blood.

Welcome to 9/11 from a New Yorker's point of view.
I'm sick and tired of statistics that explain away
those towering pillars of smoke on my horizon.

They say—
more folks die in car wrecks every year
and—
we lost more in the Second World War
even those I can't believe—
think how many we've killed in Iraq

but I thought it was on American soil that
they were all killed—
to America that they brought the fight.
Three guys in my neighborhood didn't come home that night.

You brush it off—
conspiracy theory—
and my answer to you:
where were *YOU*?
You saw it on the news
on a faceless TV screen.
It was too far away
to hurt *you*.

I looked out my bedroom window at exactly 9:47 a.m.
You couldn't know how good war sounded right then
couldn't know how I wanted to fight.
Three guys in my neighborhood didn't come home that night

and I think to myself
what did I do to them?
what did we do to them?
what did those three do to them?
and it was such a gut-wrenching, nauseating, sickening sight
that night
those three guys . . .
they still haven't come home.

Lauren Badua

Mezcal Circle

Through the large glass
that opens to doors
my patio
the horizon
a movie of blue
a mass of purple
the Sandias—
picture perfect moment
priceless

Living on a street
named after an
alcoholic drink
"yo quiero una bebida"
Mezcal
quiet neighborhood
Mezcal Circle

The large
stucco wall
takes up the majority
of the place
past the wall
a wooden cabin
surrounded by
green
a pecan tree

a plum tree
flowers
sunflowers—
a cheerful scene

Down the street
the principal cruisin' strip hosts
lowriders
souped up ten grand
waiting for a night of fun
deafening music
exchanging numbers
the whistling and honking
of a beautiful woman walking
the distant howl of sirens
night lives on
Route 66
Central

The vacant lots
used to be filled with life
neighbors
now just mere emptiness
the opportunity to exchange drugs
customers pull up
like a drive-up window
"Would you like fries with that?"

Children play on scooters
race down the slope
the asphalt guides the wheels

the screams of laughter
as they reach the bottom

The traveling scent of
chicken
pizza
floats to my nostrils
on
Mezcal Circle

My neighborhood
north of
Route 66 ■

Paul S. Hoeg

Green Chile Stew

chile
beans
meat
and broth
all come together
to form a bond
so pure
so true—
green chile stew

with pleasure
my family
will devour
this treasure—
my green chile stew

they say it's the best
how?
why?
I only follow the recipe
yet
it pleases my family

my green chile stew
my New Mexican culture

Robyn Ruff-Wagner

Fear

funny
I'm not afraid of you
but as the adult, you are afraid of me
the teenager.

you refuse to look me straight
in the eye
hypnotic.
you are scared you might
stumble over your own truth
within me
and won't be able to pick yourself up.

you nurture your nightmares
keep them alive.
death is the unknown, and you fear that, too.

while you live in your perfect sitcom world
I am shattering the TV screen
taking the wires and electronics apart to see how they work
in this process called expression
poetry
something you were never good at.

jealous, you patronize me
dub me inferior
because you're still afraid.

you take my poetry and call it
an art project
a craft
but a craft is where everyone follows the same directions
and all end up looking the same
no confusion
except for mine.

your eyes scan my face and finally settle on my blue orbs
and they are locked there
until you avert your eyes
for fear of getting lost. ■

Samantha Innis

Bleed Through

(response to Tinta y Sangre *by Ray Martin Abeyta, National Hispanic Cultural Center, Permanent Collection)*

An Asian girl won't look at me.
She hides her intellectual mind and
she's lost in
a lie.
Her perfect hips and curves and
tattoos are dreamt up quickly and
are done as she goes.
Because she knows
where babies come from. She has aborted nine out of
nine.
She knows a nun is
ready to
sell the Asian girl's soul to
God
over an anorexic fraction of tree.
Her rosary is too long and will soon snake around the
Asian girl and choke her to
freedom.
The demon above is God and
he has stolen her public flower.
Her hair is worn up to allow the jade-green empty flower truth
and crucifixion.
And because He is ever forgiving
she is led
to freedom.

Sonja Chacon

no one noticed the night
above skyline
when baby girl screamed sugar
rolling sweetness off her tongue
onto bashful landscape
so full of unreplenished nutrients
it took advantage of this indulgence
forcing its fruit to ripen too soon

and this immature seedling
hid
while revolving sunsets and sunrises
made every speck of dust sparkle
like the pink lily juice
I bathe in every morning
along w/those
baby-come-get-me
skintight jeans

forgetting that
I come from moonstone
spit from a curandera's lips
woven outta momma's womb
and rope splinters gave me her reflection

I have pieces of sun shards in my eyes
after weeping women shattered the sun
and created life w/its
scattered existence

was built on countrysides
and foothills of mountains
river mist frozen in frost
caught off guard

prayers curve my face
and fly off my hips
like religion don't stand a chance
I begin to notice
how metaphors
hang on sexual innuendoes nowadays
but it's all good

everything must be eye candy/appealing
and Maybelline says I am pretty
as long as I buy their products
b/c I wasn't born with it
tie in curling mousse and volumizing hair spray
and here I am
a nice perfectly packaged embodiment
of insecurities

chasing the moon
after women
who flirt w/their youth
and can still make
light flicker off their hips
pouring dance
on walls
till the world is completely surrounded
in their brilliance ■

Stephen Juarez

Better Days

As I stare into the mirror
This child I see
Has conjured his own problems and fears into a monster.
He's running, thinking
If someone had raised him right this wouldn't be happening.
He's blaming his mother
For the substance abuse he once endured.
He blames his father for all the physical
Beatings that have forever scarred his heart and body.
Blaming his nana is part of all the emotional guilt and
Constant wondering, who am I? and am I ugly?
Thinking of suicide was men conned by his older sister.
I step back and realize this child has yet grown into myself today.

Tamara Bryan

Origins

I come from
a nuclear family
American sitcom perfection
the surface
like an eggshell
smooth and firm

I come from a classroom
deep in the middle of the rows
quiet and huddled behind shiny textbooks with dry sentences and
a bright "A" outshines my true emotions
until even I need an outlet to discover myself

I come from a nuclear family
with a deceptive
brittle shell
cracked
poured into a bowl
the soft runny center
exposed
when a piece of the shell
split
from the whole

I come from my poetry
creating myself as I create
words that were beautiful
long before I learned to speak them
but newly discovering them brings me closer to my truth

I come from egg white
yolk streaming through the fragmented shell of
tradition
as the inside
valuable
exposed
only to myself
gathers in my palm
a broken mess that I try to absorb with my words
and make whole again ■

Mikaela Jae Renz

Sister Space

We're using the Internet now
to solve family problems—
the sisters fighting
in fiber-optic waves.

One step removed from the passion
that causes us to hurt
our words are chosen
spell-checked
clinical in their therapeutic jargon
that belies the seriousness
of the cancer
our chronic defensiveness
lodges in our bodies.

At best
we love carefully
gingerly
with fingertips and toepads
pressed to baby-bird shells
in minefields of good-intention tulips.

We are mind-sets and memories.
Our relationships stagger into the present
from the drunken, repetitive
beatings of our pasts
woven together with verbal fisticuffs
and a hollow disregard for the reality
of a sister's lived nightmare
that never resembled our own.

Our bodies, separate and unequal,
absorbed the family horrors
in three separate ways:
blocked, volleyed, relayed.

We circle each other and spar
now on the attack
now crouching
now unreachable.

We hunger. We are carnivores.
We eat each other—
our bellies never full.

All the while
we hold fast
our true-to-life faith
that we can know ourselves
without each other
know our past
without pain
confront our demons
without shedding the ones dressed
in hand-me-down sibling clothes.

We hunger. We fight.
We splinter into shadows of ourselves
and each other
until each shade of gray
becomes layered as clouds—
dark
looming
filled with unshed rain.

Receivers jammed
we listen in the silence
of an unheard future
to the typos
slipping meaning
into unknown code.

Connection lost
our words transmit one long run-on sentence
into cyberspace. ■

SHELLE VANETTEN-LUACES

My Life in 142 Words

i am:
woman, thirtysomething, mother, divorced, friend, professional,
devoted, often overwhelmed, occasionally balanced,
always curious, secretly creative and deeply in-love

i have:
older son, younger son, cozy home, purple sofa, functional car,
joy, soul mate, dream job, loving family, circle of friends, god,
along with debt, weeds, dirty dishes, stained rug, long days and short nights

i live:
early mornings, pilates, boys, driving, npr, cell phone, working, driving, knock-knock jokes, npr, boys, baths, stories, art, legos, rescue heroes, laughing, laundry, packing lunches, lullabies, thirty minutes of peace, quiet connection and late-night love

i cherish:
braxton, katon, motherhood, parents, prayer, walking, compassion, friendship, m.o.t.l.,
movies, travel, laughter, caffeine, books, chocolate, music, stillness, art, language,
little boy kisses, kindergartener conversations, saturday breakfasts, curious questions,
wine after nine, summer wind, girls' night, october mornings, old jeans and new shoes

i want:
for nothing that truly matters ■

2005

Alan Hotchkiss

Aztec Sunrise

(response to Jardin Perfumado/Perfumed Garden, *Mary Antonia Wood, 2004, Inspirados Exhibition, National Hispanic Cultural Center, 2005)*

Captured Aztec warrior,
Eyes open like the vase to his left
Looks from his pedestal,
His stony, sacrificial heart
Spurting—not blood but—
Lilies
Cascading down the side of the temple.

As lovers embrace passionately,
Soft, pink, tropical lilies fall,
Landing on their skin,
Caressing them like the soft lips
Of Chicomecoatl, Aztec goddess
Of fertility.

In this ancient religion
Sacrifice does not mean death,
But rather the birth
Of the Morning Lily. ■

Alicia Leger

My Voice

My voice is what I say
My voice is what *you* choose to hear

It demands you believe a certain lie
"The earth is flat
And *center* of the universe"

My voice soothes
Hides
Questions

It can trigger a tsunami
Flooding through your mind

A liar's word whispered
A dictator's word shouted

Can you hear me?
Secrets behind a wrinkled hand
Weapons of mass destruction
Good excuse
Good war

Without my voice where would I be?
Cocooned inside my quiet mind
Unable to break free

A lone person
On the curb
Wildly thinking
Yet silently watching

But my voice erupts out
Freeing me from thought
And thrusting me into a world that will hear me

Ana Romero

Soldados

Son soldados
o son veteranos,
pero al final luchando como hermanos.

Para qué luchan soldados?
No lo dudamos . . .
defienden su estado,
su tierra querida, tan enriquecida de petróleo, de oro,
y gente mala con todo.

Matan a enfermos,
matan a malos,
matan a niños desamparados,
a gente inocente que nada entiende,
que solo viven en un cruel presente.

Cuestionen a su presidente
que mata sin motivo,
que solo piensa en su presente
y en su futuro maligno.

¿Por qué no lo aceptan?
La vida sin guerra es mejor,
especialmente si estamos unidos,
y vivimos sin rencor.

Demi Olivas

American "Lover"?

Quetzalcoatl is a snake
a scaled line who eventually
curls back
to devour his own tail for infinity

my bowed fetus grew up
to do somersaults
toes in mouth
gnawing
down
self

while still confronting learned social biological cycles:

an attraction across energy memory space
chemically pulling me to men
like you

I remember that sensation
Is it dad or America?
I take your hand

I'm afraid of
it
not you

though I spread wide
a dick diverts my focus

I resist chewing my toes at lotus position dawn

I am resurrection sunrises away
from the pottery studio

with you I neglect
networked
space

with you I won't transform this poem into beauty
that would be like a somersault ■

Emilio Juri

Argentina

Argentina, linda
y querida

Que lástima
que estés
tan herida

por culpa
de ese ex-presidente
que no supo
quererte.

Eres tan linda,
tu calles llenas de
mujeres en sus vestidos de domingo
que no sé
por que te
castigan.

Eres tan verde,
tus árboles se estiran para
alcanzar la luz del sol
que en otoño
todo se muere.

Tus lagos son lindos
como brazos abrazando
las montañas
Lástima el gentío

que contamina
el agua
con puro
desperdicio.

Hay días felices,
platicando con mi amiga de pelo
largo y negro en la
esquina de Malagueño y Richeri
aunque algunos
son tristes
comiendo rápido en el suelo
antes de dejar Argentina.

No importa el lugar
toda será
como tú
lo quieras
pintar.

Yo aprendí
que lejos
de ti
lograría conseguir
un mejor futuro
para mí
una chance de crecer
como un hambriento volcán.

Aquí estoy
en este país
tratando de llenar

mis bolsillos de oro
lejos de ti.

Me di cuenta
que más nunca recordaría
tus calles
en las
que yo
viví.

Regresaré orgulloso
a mi querido país
solo a visitarte.

En mis manos como
las de un hombre,
leo mi futuro de vida
en otro lado. ■

Julian Godinez

What You See Is Me

What you see is me.
Yes, I am preppy and an athletic sports fan.
"You're just some dumb white boy."
But that ain't the truth at all,
because I'm not white, I'm Mexican,
with everything in between.
Just because I dress a certain way,
do a certain activity,
doesn't mean you know me.
I am as a rose before it blooms.
As the green bud starts to sprout,
a color comes very soon.
Just because my color's white
doesn't mean my color has bloomed.
I am everything you can think of
from black to white
and brown to blue.

MARY FERGUSON

Loco L.A.

A sweet old lady inside her quaint little house looks out into her part of the neighborhood. I remember Grandma's house in Avenue, can still see the tags all over the place. Avenue was right next door to my neighborhood. Joyful kids play in the streets, their parents watching them like hawks.

The picture: cholos and cops around the corner. The death of a homie right before my eyes. "Friends for life," my father told him as a little vato in the streets. It changed my view on life, kept me out of the blood-filled streets, helped me to make something of my life instead of screwing up like a lot of my friends did.

'Til this day, for just a few weeks, when I go back to Avenue and my old neighborhood to see my grandma, my grandpa, my family and friends, I remember that picture when looking at each tag, thinking of my life in East L.A. ■

Nick Etre

Another Four Years of Fear

Public transmissions filter through faces and biased opinions.
No friend I can trust, just a chance to boost myself above.
The disorder and the order compose my charcoal-faded dove.

Spoiled and selfish, the cowboy reigns
With a little red phone in the drawer of his oil-plated desk.
He buys his way through life with the little green bill that he covets most.
No, this is not an environmental act.

I don't need oxygen.
I need a shiny new Ford with some tinted windows,
Because when I look outside, there are truths I can't handle.

But as we connect, others disconnect,
Living in their persistent comfortable seclusion from life.

What weapons of mass destruction?
Oil is all we stole, I mean found.
I wouldn't want to doubt our president's judgment; that would be heresy.
We all know what happens to threats.

The smiley face rolls back prices.
At least he got the rich a tax cut; they needed that.

I was a child once, and I was left behind,
Deceived into thoughts of honesty.
Well, promises were broken, as were the alliances we used to share.
The people of our own country know less than those we are invading.

Flags flurry in a soldier's hand in another's country.
We bomb Baghdad civilians for a war on terror.

The red terror alerts keep me awake at night.
We impose our beliefs because we must be right.
To create peace we must fight.

I want to be free.
Free from a family full of fascists sometimes residing in Texas.
Free from fear of mushroom clouds filling the air.
Free from the lack of freedom. ■

Samantha Innis

Hello, New York

Hello, New York.
This is your mother speaking.
Didn't you get my message?
Didn't you know I called?
Didn't you see the twisted
look on my face
when I asked you how you were doing?

Hello, New York.
It's me again.
I just wanted to check up on you.
I just wanted to check in with you.
I just wanted to let you know
I had been thinking about you.

Hello, New York.
I thought I'd leave a note.
To tell you that there is no preference.
To tell you that there are no ends.
To tell you that there is no hope
for what seems to be our future.

Hello, again, New York.
This will be my last message.
I just felt I had to say that you were my only dream.
I just felt I had to say that I was the last one here.
I just felt I had to let you know that I once was
Lady Liberty and I was dressed in gold.

Mikaela Jae Renz

Peddling in Barelas

What they sell
we buy
resisting in stolen moments
of intimacy between the races.

I ride through Barelas—
bridge between
South Valley Pride
and
we-can-never-admit-we-have-history-unless-it-brings-tourists
downtown—
toward home.

I pass hermanos y hermanas
smile
shy wave
to say:
hola—buenas dias—gracias—
I'm fighting, too.

Pedaling in the sunshine
I labor to push forward
a world with
no work force
only *work with*

My resistance:
to see people
to see structure

to understand
to use my body and my hands and my days
to hold back the collapsing walls
of global culture that say:
you can only buy freedom
consume and be consumed.
there is no connection beyond transaction
and the hand that feeds you
will teach you the limit of love.

My love holds out the possibility
of dignity
integrity
culture not out of a box.

The neighborhoods I pass
hold themselves together
with woven cords.

I work with
those who would fight
for their right to stay. ■

SHELLE VANETTEN-LUACES

What's New

I met
Two friends
To catch up
On what's new

Jodi just moved
Their new house
Because
Their three children
Each need space—
3000 square feet
Was not enough

Wendy just bought
Her fourth new car
In four short years
Because
They have four priorities
A convertible for fun
A minivan for car pools
An SUV for weekends
The Mercedes for business

I sit, listening, sipping red wine
They compare notes on architects
And built-in DVD players

Eventually, they turn to me
Asking enthusiastically
"What's new with you?"

A quick mental inventory:
One fixer-upper
One old car
One challenging job
One true love
Two beautiful boys . . .

Quietly, I answer . . .
"Same old stuff." ■

2006

Alyssa Garcia

I want to tell them everything that happened that first night I didn't come home,
but I can't.

I know they'll say it wasn't my fault, but every day I think about what I could've
done to take myself out of that position, so it is my fault.

I shouldn't have been there at all, but life in all its sincerity was lying to me,
and time was pushing me to a place I never wanted to see.

I had no control.

Fourteen years old seemed so secure, but I grew up with the people who used
white powder dreams religiously, and it was only a matter of time
before their dreams were mine too.

My best friend of the night gave me something I want to hide from the
innocent and naïve, because it's what their parents told them happened
to the girls they warned them about.

That was only the beginning, and they really don't want to know the truth
about a high school girl getting "taken advantage of," as they like to put it.

But it's real, and I know now it was my fault for making him want to be the
villain in my life of heroes and secret societies.

He can't give back what he took away from me that night, so perfect everywhere
else but the room he locked me in to pretend everything was OK.

The light was darker than anything, and his once-bright eyes were a color of insanity that I never want to see again.

Through the sound of ripping clothes, I can hear what I should be saying but can't, because my voice was being strangled by fear.

He says sorry, but it means nothing.

I KNOW it was my fault. I should've done what I said I always would.

The best high ever is the worst memory when my truths became jokes that no one i laughing at.

I know I'm scaring my loyalist alibis by my carelessness, but they don't get it.

I don't understand myself. Living in reality is a waste of time. I don't care that it takes so long to see what's right in front of me.

I love that he gave me the ability to see what I was too afraid of. I only wish he would have done it in a different way, because I've spent three years killing mysel

My promise to my only truth has been a lie.

I'm sorry I made him want to do it.

But I just want to tell them what happened that first night I didn't come home.

Anthony "WonderBoy" Alaniz

My America

My America simmers—a fantasy locked between these small ears of mine.
The reality is a concrete rain forest where I see broken glass and candy wrappers
littering the
streets.
Street cracks leak their way into buildings, decay the structures surrounding
the glorious Staples Center.
Faceless somebodies walk by faceless nobodies.
The only faces peer out from advertisement billboards.
Angelina Jolie asks, "Got Milk?"
I've got my milk, buddy-d.
Thank you very much, Angelina Jolie.

Wait, stop.
Take a step back with me and look through the decayed building cracks.
Peer into my mind to see flowers blooming in clear waters.
Tree leaves dance with the air free from exhaust fumes.
I lie in a field filled with daisies, and I'm smiling.
My fantasy struggles to slither out through the holes, materialize my mind's dream
in this reality, destroy the steel wall confines where my fantasy and my reality
can become one:
My America.

Antonio Rael

La Muerte de un Loco

(response to La muerte de un loco*, Alejandro Colunga, 1984, National Hispanic Cultural Center, 2006)*

You feel the evil of Satan within.
It takes over all good and puts itself in.
God is now a Deathlike figure, and Angels are Demons.
You feel the good of everything in heaven
get sucked out like
a vacuum cleaner sucking
shit out of your carpet.
Darkened Skies filled with fire
show that evil's presence is with us all around.
The Father, The Son, and The Holy Ghost
all just seem to be another thought blown away
like a tumbleweed blown
yard by yard in the windy high desert.
The only sign of brightness
has its own satanic way.
The shadowed faces show
that evil has set good aside and taken
its spot on the throne of domination for the century.
Where is all good?
Where has all hope gone?
There is no more turning around and hiding from the reality
because it's in your mind forever.

You are going to face the creatures
and embrace what the face has to say as it looks
you directly in the eye
its skeleton covered with rag-like old clothes.
Darkness has imprisoned me
in the painting with the
fiery face waving the mysterious flag.
Darkness dwells over me as it
flies through the black clouds and fire-covered sky.
All that we have now is the prayer for tomorrow
if there is a possibility for a tomorrow . . . ■

Bianca Lopez

I carry the bones of my brother that have not yet, nor will they ever, change.
Ashes to ashes, dust to dust: things not of his final state.
The bones grow heavier when soaked with alcohol and tears from stale memories,
but suppression of life-destroying, soul-smashing grief and veneer smiles
will lift them off my shoulders for a brief moment
so I can take my shallow breaths of despair.
That twelve-year-old life taken too soon will descend from the split grey sky
on soft silken wings fit for him
and release the bones like his casket into the earth
to remind me that I am mortal and must live the life he didn't.
I carry the bones of my brother
once filled with the blood of his parents and rebellious marrow,
now flooded with tears of family members never met,
and a portion of my never-decomposing adoration. ■

Carlos Contreras

Common ground

(written in conversation with Diane Thiel's "The Minefield")

1

We found ourselves,
some two generations   apart.
Not much in common,
still we'd played cat's cradle
with the same *trip wires.*

2

She must have been young then.
Those stories ricocheting off her ears like enemy fire
off fellow fighters—
did it hurt?
I want to ask her . . .
Did you . . .
cry?
Knowing of the silence
wrapped like pine boxes in burdened banners,
but we were just pajama feet
POWs

Did it hurt?

3

Not when he hit but . . .
when he . . .
spoke?

I wouldn't be trying to
find out
more about her
as much as I would be
about myself;
like I said, we were generations
apart.
I haven't had time for my
heart to honorably discharge
my childhood memories.

4
Seems our fathers
shared common
ground—
defined themselves
with enemy lines
and never crossed too far
when recanting over dinner.

Mine
never snapped—
exploded on the inside
instead.
Like pigeons after an
Alka-Seltzer Breakfast,
his heart came home
but his mind never left it.

5
She may want to ask me,
did it hurt?
Not when he spoke,
but when he . . .
slept?
And we can compare stories

"My dad would throw things,
noisy fm radios at kitchen walls."
"Mine would have slept through a fire in
the living room."
Both fighting
fire with fire.
We'd know there was
no honorable discharge.
There is no way of assigning
demerits for angry
actions at this point because
Reality is
MIA.
Defeat is begging on the
Corner
and somehow
They are still
Home.

6
Home,
a place where battlefields still exist,
and we've
taken off the pajamas
and adorned fatigues
because if there is
anything worth fighting for, it is them

7
She and I
may never know exactly
what happened—
where the mines within them
are hidden
and just what it takes
to explode.

Demi Olivas

Starlight quivers between
A light piano key there
My nerves wave
Your hips are a soft voice wooing through the telephone wire

I'm the pigeon watching
and the woman in the window on top of you

Hombre
I would gently cup my fingers around your eyes to stop them from wandering
but then I'd be driving to crash

You're a bright Aztlan bird flapping its wings
splashing your feathers against city walls
eating worms disguised as eagles or priests . . .
you land on telephone wires to strum songs

. . . and my ego will feed you if you promise to come back

but me, right now
I feel like only one red corn and an aloe vera plant that I forgot to water and killed
I have little to give
but mostly my devotion to lend what I earn

Hombre, I'm a poor bruja
and if my body is a bag to gather medicine
I've built up religious rhetoric, good intentions, less *now* than next, and plenty of pheromones

My altar is full of things given to me
My prayers sit in a gallery and sometimes get on stage

My cat ran away

The only eagle feather I have is the one you gave me
The only song I sing is a mantra because I don't believe in my words
See man, I am as small as a man who feels big

but my bag is mostly breath
full of hope

If I woman am land and you man are sky
then this big city asses faults between us

We argue because I expect rain you don't carry in the pockets of your glands

I am a potter
I can carry water
I know where the river is

I want to thank you for shaking the cage of my demons
Yes!
they are drama queens dressed in tears

They come out of my mouth and blame you
This is exactly what mother did to father

and your bright wings droop into hanging glue tape
with dead flies on your dark spots when you sulk from my saltiness

so that day I got in my car to leave you forever after I made love to you one
last time
and the battery of my car died

my heart didn't stop

but my battery did
that feeling I used to watch from the telephone wire

Hombre, if I leave now I'll go home
where they draw Jesus like a white European man
and use their bible highlighter to trace his path
numbering each stop as verses

and sitting *there*
with *"they"*

I'll miss your shaggy muppet hair

because you don't know how to count very well
You accept only zero
not the number
not the shape that cycles sky and land
but Now

Hombre, I am not the earth, I'm not that big and round and you're not that blue or wet
That fantasy the wise people told me died because you did not water it

Hombre,
I am living inside a square
that's inside a circle
Have compassion for me
and I'll stop tripping if you start life cycling
until I learn to stop ■

Elissa Hutson

Childhood

Her hands slowly braided my wispy blonde hair underneath the scorching June sun, her fingers weaving back and forth rhythmically as she hummed an old Spanish song and tapped her shoeless feet against the hot red bricks outside. The smell of sweat and sweet vanilla perfume mixed with the summer breeze as I studied the intricate lines of her hands. They were rough from years of hard work, worn from too many exhausting days, weathered from working in the sun. But as her skin swept softly across my head, her touch soothed me; it was like being wrapped in a fleece blanket and rocked to dreamland. I reached my tiny porcelain hands out to hers, as if I could capture all of her experiences with just a touch of my fingertips.

This is how I recall many of my childhood days. My dad hired her to take care of us when I was just six months old. She had the responsibility of caring for three troublesome boys and one little girl from nine until four every day of the week. For as long as I can remember, she was the one who played hide and seek with me, covered my cuts with Sesame Street Band-Aids, fed me waffles in the bathtub as I splashed playfully in the soapy water.

"Come on, Chiquita. Let's go inside for lunch," she said as she kissed the top of my head with her cracked lips.

She made us sandwiches—the kind cut into little shapes with cookie cutters and have no crust—as my brother and I set out to make a fort. We combined a blue Batman blanket that he stripped from his bed and a plethora of lacy pink pillows that I took from my doll's crib to create a playhouse in the middle of the living room.

"Delivery," she said as she tapped on our newly crafted castle.

"Password," my brother said condescendingly, a toothless grin on his freckled face.

She smiled as she peered between the cushions and placed the flower-printed paper plate beside us to share. ■

Esmé Vaandrager

Two Voices: Hendrik, Esmé.

(6.12.6)

This shit is gonna be crazy.
The night is in our hands,
Stuffed in our pockets, burning slow
From the puckered tips of cigarettes.
Smoke catches the moonlight,
Ash and sky mixing in our chests as we take our smoldering fill
Strongly, easily.

Baby boy ain't so baby no more.
He's a tall thing,
Stretched out and long-legged,
Grown a bit from two sticks poking up from big feet,
Marking territory—
Yes, it would hurt his feelings if he heard that.

I can't help but feel like a rock star.
Super boys
Flopped jaunty against the wall,
Glaring coolly through our hair,
Ready for nothing
Short of fun.

His hands surprise me.
They resemble my father's.
I want to hold him,
Big sister coming up to his shoulder
Or his chin.

We haven't marked that difference exactly
'Cos these roles are always changing,
Switching faces.

Light another.
I feel the need to make a mark tonight,
To slice through the air
And examine the rip I leave,
Pull at its edges
And see if it can open any bigger.

We take turns being mad at each other.
I can't help but feel worried,
Shaken from a comfort spot where I was the bad one
Leading the way responsibly into trouble,
Making sure nothing went too wrong,
Always able to call you baby
Because I had things to teach you.

I like to fix things.
　　Rather, make things happen.
I like to make things work and keep how I did it a secret.
My favorite times with my grandfather were
The times he taught me magic tricks.
Power lies in not letting people know the right button,
The finger slipped under the deck momentarily,
In not letting them not need you
To make the illusion complete.

I am surprised by the story of the condom breaking,
Your questions about pills
Breaking surfaces I never associated with you.
You know I'll always want to help,

I want lots of people at my funeral.
I want there to be a crater,
A vacuum I used to fill.

Grateful for a chance to be a part of your life
Because I am so scared that . . .

Water moves by the moon.

The world moves by our reactions to it.

I am young and as close to invincible as I'll ever be,
So we won't talk about tornadoes
Or shit we can't control.
The air is twistable,
And what you don't want to be in the air,
You can twist out,
Fold under,
Ignore,
Mock.

I feel sick,
Exhausted from clutching icy, crumpled worries in my stomach,
Startled that so quickly
I will find you to be a man—
And I still with my need to hold you.

This shit is gonna be crazy. ■

Faustino Villa

My reasons to live are not so big. They are only four and seven years old, something I will adore until the game of life is over. I will give 'em what I have and more, because when I was dead, they woke me up and said, "Can I make him some toast or bread?"

"How about you join me to some Fruity Pebbles and defeat the devils?" He does what I do, because I am considered someone cool, watching the Saturday morning cartoons, where imagination runs wild, turning a stick into a sword and touching the stars.

There are galaxies far away, but if you can play with G.I. Joes, you're considered to be one of the bros, screaming out loud, "all aboard," because we're going to munch with Cap'n Crunch, and we'll be back in time for lunch. ■

Jesse James

I should've danced stronger
I should've flirted harder
I should've talked longer

A mere hug wasn't nearly enough to quench my thirst for him

We danced, hugged, and that was it

I said, "I love the way you dance"
He replied, "It's always nice to see you"

I think that was backwards. I've held his attention for longer with fewer words and more moves, and I was the one in awe every time I saw him.

Eyes like a desert storm, that one, mysterious and comforting.

To hide a blush, I continued dancing
I gave him a token of my excitement—
A dollar store ring
A rose of all things
It flashed with the same sporadic capacity my heart does in his presence

Next time
Next time . . . I'll dance with him not next to him but with him
On him, I'll make sure he knows he misses me and wants me before the night is over

Joe Romero

Abuela, I'm sorry for forgetting
Where I come from

I'm sorry for not knowing
Our native tongue

And I'm sorry for not realizing what
You and abuelo went through
To get me where I am today

I am a Mexican
Not Hispanic, Latino or Chicano

Dad, your parents are from Mexico
Not Hispania

Fuck you, don't ever call me boy
My family raised a fuckin' man

Dad told me I'm not Mexican
My bloodline tells me different

My skin is that of a Mexicano
And I'm sorry for not working
Twelve-hour days just to stay poor

Grandpa, I'm sorry you had to raise
A nine-person family on a one-person budget
I'm sorry I had to leave you
But mama needed me

Mama, I'm sorry for not being able to
Stop dad when he needed to relieve
Some stress

I'm sorry you got addicted to addiction

No, do not apologize for the life you gave me
I'm sorry for the life I gave you

I'm sorry for fucking up the life
You gave me

I'm sorry for the bruises

Nothing but opportunity in front of me
and I'm sorry for not taking advantage

It's time to start making some changes

Abuela, I remember where we come from
Dirt . . . lived in Barelas near the tracks
And made something of yourselves
And you knew Spanish

Grandpa, I had to go, mama needed me

Mama, dad's gone now, and the bruises
Have faded

And there's nothing else to apologize for
I love you ■

Julio Mendez and Sara Samani

Writing a New Book

Julio & Sara: I'm six years old

Julio: drinking beers, drinking beeersss . . .

Sara: watching Nickelodeon, hating the color orange

Julio & Sara: Seven

Sara: finding out my mom's favorite color is orange

Julio: chillin' by the river around the fire cooking *carnitas* around the disco

Julio & Sara: I'm eight years old

Julio: holding cookies for my dad so the cops don't search me

Sara: realizing I look good in orange

Sara: fifteen

wearing an orange life jacket

Julio & Sara: Nine

Sara: still hating orange

Julio: *kiquiándole con mis padrinos en peña blanca*

Sara: eleven

the ice melts and the sky kisses me,
they call it "raining"

Julio & Sara: Seventeen

Sara: cold and wet. The life jacket didn't work.

Julio: tippin' over on that liquor. Tell me, is this right to do or naw not even?

Sara: twelve

disliking the taste of fish

Julio & Sara: Thirteen

Julio: "HOMEBOY! HOW YOU BEEN, *PUTO*?"
"*Q'VOLE 'UEY, SACA LA MOTA, CABRÓN*—BLAZE IT UP!"
A week later caught with a knife at school and on probation

Sara: wanting to be a big white fish

Julio & Sara: At fourteen

Sara: I'm sitting on the aqua-tiled sides of a pool

Julio: I became an alcoholic, by choice, slinging weed on the streets
I come up with a dime and make it into a bill.
Stacking benjis

Julio & Sara: I'm ten years old

Julio: baking cookies, learning to cook and sell

Sara: trying to kiss the sky's ice, but too short to reach

Julio & Sara: Sixteen

Sara: planning a trip to the mountain's ice-cream cone point

Julio: big balling, slinging rock on the avenue,
packing a .22 with a mini nine
living the life of a rap star without the deal or studio

Julio & Sara: Today . . .

Sara: I'm as dry as a book with too many pages

Julio: I'm writing in a new book, shutting an old one

Lauren Brenner

Ode to My Bed

You, my dear, harbor me nightly. You hold me close and wrap me tightly.
You, covered in greens and pinks and stripes of white, are my bed.
You host the vacations and blurry dreams in my head.
I fall into you after long nights of drinking and thinking
And you never let me hit ground. You catch me.
(Except for that one time three months ago when you let me slide off
The edge and hit my head, you asshole, and wake with a cough.)
When I am depressed, I lay on you, and you keep me safe.
I have hour-long phone conversations while I suffocate you.
We talk of him and another boy named him and that girl named she
And how he and she can be so cruel, but the other, he means well.
You don't need to understand. Actually, I'd rather have you not understand.
Bed, I hope the only language you know is Chinese,
Because if you have English ears, then you know me too well.
I hope your eyes are always closed, bed, or else you have seen
Too many of my tears, and watched nights with my guests turn obscene.
I am lazy, bed, and you know this well. I work you too hard—
Usually twelve hours a day, but you don't complain.
I love you, bed. I miss you right now. I want to freeze time and visit you.
I want to jump into you and never crawl through.
I want to burrow between you and my green wall—and maybe,
This time I won't wake up with thumbtacks in my thigh.
I need to clean you out, bed! You are *so* dirty. Clean yourself.
I wash your sheets, but you always allow scissors and tape
To spend the night with me—I don't like sleeping with inanimate objects.
But in the end, bed, we've been through it all:
Sleepovers and popcorn kernels and dogs that have died;
Friends who slept here have now moved away,
But we remain constant. The only action you guarantee me
Is the shutting of my eyes, and my ability to dream. ■

Lenell Storey

This is home
Culture packaged neatly
In cinder block houses,
Curved lines in cubist perspective.
The light bounces.
Shapes shift
Around us
Blended bodies
Blended people
Blended families
Collaged
Not catalogued
By borders that have
Tried to define us.

The lines in the road
Are designed to keep us safe
But the law of averages
Demands collision.
In a perfect moment in time
What stories will be written
When our planes of existence intersect?

An open mouth
Dissertation from an
Old man
Reminds us of old ways
And tells us how he appreciates the changes.

He kept
Grandma's tortilla recipe

Written on a piece of cardboard
From a cracker box
Sacred.
He thinks it is important
His grandchildren
Speak Spanish and not get beaten.

His words were never as strong as
What he taught with—
Sunrises
On mornings after the cries
From branded calves
And the acrid scent of burning hair
Had died away
Or when boiling water scalded the skin
Of a fattened pig
And warmed the air
In November.
Chicharones and liver
Were fruits we ate only from Matanzas.

We are not limited by
Farm upbringings.
MBAs and PhDs
Were birthed from the same river
As drug dealers and drunks,
All of it quilted in fields
Sustained by wire fencing
And irrigation canals.

Water bubbles with the
Fear that coyotes will attack
The newborn calf in the night.

This rich land
Grew so many different
Crops tall and strong.
It synthesized
Cyclic creation.
Living words envisioned in daily life
Evolved from snake pits
And surgical discovery.

Heaven sends sunlight
To take advantage of our skin
And bless us with forgiveness,
Sacrament of water and breath.

Don't judge me a heretic
As I pray over other cultures' corpses.
They came in search of
The heaven-sent light
And big sky inspiration—
Daily bread for their families
Not prisoners' rations,
Immigrating to the banks of
The river looking for new air to breathe,
Different hues of skin.

We all deserve salvation.

Martín Montaño-Pilch

Innocence

When the bright, white-blue lightning's shout is too loud, when the wind blows too hard, when the shadow of the night stretches too far—that's innocence: finding fear in the crack of thunder, the howl of the wind, then comfort in your mother's arms, in the warmth that radiates from the little folds of the sheets on your parents' bed.

I think it was raining that night. Little glistening droplets were falling from the stars. Huge thunderclouds were drifting heavily toward us, barely clinging to the cargo they held, just barely holding on to the rain. I remember it was pretty late; the night was edging over the hills, the sun coasting into the horizon. It is innocent to fear the darkness under the clouds, the lightning and the thunder. The beauty of the storm was overthrown by my fear of it.

Beauty

shifted.

It was a surprise party, for him, my best friend, and then, I don't know how to describe it, but she was there. I don't really know who she was. I heard rumors—fables—of her, but I didn't know what to expect. Soon, I found out.

When you chisel off the layers of her personality, the complexity of her free spirit, when you get down to the way she existed in the room, she was sexy—not because her body was curved, her lips so perfect, her eyes bright blue—but because her mouth was always smiling, her eyes always dancing with wonder and mischief, her voice never afraid to laugh. I'm a sucker, a sap, such a damn fool to love her.

I think it's innocent when the sun dips into the horizon, setting the sky streaming red and dark, and you're afraid. I think it's innocent when the only thing that says sex is the chart that asks if you're a guy or a girl, or when the only thing that is horny is the rosebush; the only thing with a kiss is the little Hershey's chocolates. Then there's Holly.

I don't think I've looked a girl in the eye for longer than five seconds. Usually it's the cop-a-glance, look away, look back, look away, but no, not now. I actually talked to her, looked her in the eye, and what's more amazing—she listened, and I listened to her. She laughed at my jokes; I laughed at hers. I'm young: love is a foreign concept; growing up is mystery.

It was raining that night. The thunder was booming, but I know I wasn't scared. It's innocent to be scared of the mosaic of flashing light, but I wasn't. I was with Holly, and the thunder wasn't the roar of the dark clouds anymore, but the batting of her eyelashes. The lightning wasn't the fury of the stars, but the electricity that flowed through our bodies. It's innocent to find comfort in Mom's arms. I don't know what it is when a girl finds comfort in yours. I think . . . I think it's love. ■

Matthew Meyer

The Average High/The Academy Was . . .

I'm perfect I know it!
I'm perfect I know it!
I'm perfect. I know it isn't just me who needs it.

I'm the answer to the question that blooms in her mind, and
I'm the metaphorical coke line that makes her eyes shine.
She holds my hands and not only makes me feel beautiful but
Tells me that I'm her world in Spanish,
So I can't understand it,
But I know she's saying it.
I can see it in her dripping closed eyes. I know it.
I can feel it every time I commit a lip-shared lie.
I know it because I'm perfect,
Because in her dreams I already am and have to be,
Never wrong always right, that's right.
That's me, I'm always . . .

Right back to that day when I'm face to face with the man
Who tells me
I need to get my shit together.
A face that no longer resembles my loving father,
He talks in a tone so deep that words could have gone right through me,
His passive arms turned violent over my future.
I explain, "I'll do better."
Holding things inside each and every blink of my eye
Because what he said is surely for the best.
No more perfection in my future,
No more my future, perfection's not . . .

"In my future is where I see you, love," she whispers.
Tapping out, she can't follow thoughts in her head.
The cuts dig deeper in her skin.
Steel slits deeper through her wrist.
The empty feeling is finally peeking out the cut.
It looks so morbidly beautiful.
"I love it, and I hate me . . ."
"I'm dizzy; the room's spinning; blood is falling; the razor's shining.
My arm that pays for my intake of stress screams to me, 'are we perfect yet?
Are we perfect yet, are we perfect . . .'"

Quivering after her denial of his beating,
She hopes that he isn't leaving,
Looking the other way when he's cheating.
"He loves me, he loves me, he loves me.
These bruises were only an accident . . . He didn't want to
Push me, slap me, hit me, hurt me . . . but it's breaking me . . .
It's my fault he's angry.
I didn't call him.
I was supposed to call him;
I meant to call him . . .
Our relationship is perfection,
Because he makes me perfect with every glance he gives me
And every touch he tries to love me."

I'm perfect; I know it.
I'm losing it; I know it.
But how can we say we're stretching past this ocean
If we know we're drowning in it?

Robert P. Ramirez

Twelve Voices

I want to be me,
But I feel I'm caged
Between age, race,
And the need to express.
I want to be me,
The me that thinks sex is overrated.
I would rather slide fingers over ear
And have deep conversations,
Yeah,
Teach myself to learn her soul,

But there is something else in me,
And it's ripping my morale,
Stabbing knives into backs of good conscience,
Damning them to hell.
I don't believe it,
But maybe my Gemini lies and tells secrets.

Two Persons In One Man,

Try twelve.

One loves,
And two hates.
Three is peace,
Hummingbird racing with speed through the skies,
Like sheets on the bed where I lie
And get away from my life.
Four is a vulture,
Circling, circling,
Needing to survive,
No matter the cost,
Feasting off others' purity
And making it mine.

Five is lost in cliché of hurt and pain,
Number six throws down razor blades,
And cherishes wrists.
He is sacred, and I love him,
For he reminds me most of the moons,
But there are times when my mind
Chooses what to consume,
Like seven—
He's the actor,
Pretends to be a friend like he'll sit there and listen,
But he wants more.
He wants beauty between body and naked,
What lies between the legs, not the mind, and that scares me.
What if one day I meet Ms. Right, Ms. Intellectual, Ms. Artist, Ms. Strong,
And seven comes along strutting and flaunting his swagger,
Talking about, "What's up girl?
Can I get them digits or what?"

I can't be that;
I can't be him.

Eight is always late, fashionably of course,
And one day rushing,
I might be running and trip over something
Only to
Break My Neck,
My vanity.
Then there is nine,
The type of guy to slang and steal,
Getting high and bang for real,
Bumping Gangster Rap,
Emulating Scarface,
Blue bandana around his fist.
He'll fight for money, guns, drugs or a bitch,
And any guy that can refer to feminine pride
Embraced in a human being
As a bitch,
I don't really like and don't think I can kick it with.

Ten,
Ten is monumental, marching on memorials,
Running all races onto the same platform,
Revolutionary—
Che Guevera, Pancho Villa, Emiliano Zapata—
Down for the Raza type of heavy-handed,
Lay down the law,
Robin Hood bandit,
Learn from what he saw,
What he wants he's going to have it,
Type of guy,
And don't get me wrong,
That can be cool sometimes.
Eleven embraces his cross,
Walks in the steps of Saint Francis,
Catches hope by the tail,
And twelve,
Well, twelve I'm not sure.
Like a blur of eleven colors,
Mixed and twisted into one,
Brown,
A little darker, my hair,
A little lighter, my palms,
Is this me?
All colors varied and swayed,
Different textures,
Different lights,
Different shades,
The tone and the rhythm,
The movement and balance,
Me,
I am all twelve on canvas,
Painted with beliefs. ■

Samantha Innis

Anatomy

I want to study your anatomy
Just like you study trees.
I want you to look at me like
You look at them.
Tell me about their blossoms
Their colors, their scent, the way they
Move in the wind.
Ignore my denial and say that the blossoms fall down
And not up.
Tell me all about it.
You can rant all you want, please
As you
Run your fingers through *my* roots
Make a grapevine with our fingers
Squeeze wine from me as a gift
To you, and
Study my anatomy.
I want to show you that full is just as beautiful as
Those casting linear trees
Barely catching sun amongst themselves.

I want you to see that
My curves make things your trees cannot
Silhouettes
Silhouettes
Sultry, shadowy silhouettes.
I can dance and move
Manipulate the dark
Mold it over my Junoesque curves
Resembling waterfalls and valleys
Hooking on my sides
Shoulders down
Curving slips, far too untamed
To be the slow, straight-growing trees . . .
I want you to study my anatomy
Because you cannot have a tree
Without its crows.

Sara Samani

She carries the white stick.
She is standing in the earthen tributaries,
those roots grazing electrically by her feet.
She is woman gently touching smoke with her breath.
The smoke magnetized up by a silver moon,
but damn she needs blue fire, the hottest kind.
She can spin planetarily in mariachi dress,
the paneled waves shooting orange liquid.
But damn, this girl, she needs blue fire, the hottest kind.
She is enjoying the moments that snap and tie like rubber bands,
trying to free the pages and figure why she's so electrically twirling,
lying with angles only Egyptian pyramids know
next to the summer tree, burning paper with her teeth.
The flowers glow like lava rocks.
But damn she needs blue fire, the hottest kind.
She wishes Harry Potter weren't quite so lame,
so she could love it without feeling shame,
but she's the one kissing her daughter's wrists, strong lips.
Hera's oracle, she is prophesying vengeance against a spinning earth,
the spinning in the back of a goddess's eyes,
dizzy because she is Lava's heat and Dante's temptation.
He paper clipped her silver love in photo memoir,
but damn, this woman, she needs blue fire, the hottest kind.
Vestal virgin walks straight for the moon bowl,
fire,
earth,
and air,
Though she sinks as the smoke lifts and the fire burns. ■

Mikaela Jae Renz

Weaving,
I slip knots past fabrics long ago braided,

adding the artistry of these hands
shaped by the threads they've picked up

into my pattern
of star charts with unknown destiny,

semblance of order and chaos
falling in orbits typical,

calculable,
rhythmic as heavenly bodies

exploding outward
before cosmic collapse.

Turning again to my life—
this small star cluster of moments

Venn diagrams into calendars—
schedules ruled by months not weeks,

bigger than days.
Shortly a year will seem like nothing—

a car ten years old still seems new
when I begin to fear the day

just minutes from now
when my ten-year-old daughter not yet born

will start to drive,
her own life a new path,

pulled by the gravity of objects
from a galaxy different than mine,

related, perhaps, in a shared constellation
but separate orbits.

Who will she see
spinning from center?

Gaseous planet?
Fractal exploration of her past in my edges?

A map?
Do not follow sign?

Breathing sun?
A comforting moon?

What will remain centered in me
when love spills over my horizons like rain

and I weave simultaneous threads—
partner, parent,

woman
and worker,

a teacher who remains a student
of culture and community

a poet who listens
a lover who waits to understand

a mother who praises
a girl who constantly wakes, smiling?

In a revolving, looming world,
who can tire of the view? ■

Shelle VanEtten-Luaces

Eggs

The dawn light peeked through window as she dressed in the half-light, accompanied by the rooster's morning song. Slipping out of the room, she paused to look enviously at her sister, still sleeping contentedly under the cozy, handmade quilt.

Mother was in the kitchen peeling potatoes. Father's thermos was gone—he had already left for the fields. She greeted her mother with a quiet kiss before she walked out the back door. For a moment, she imagined what it would feel like to keep walking, out the yard, down the dirt road . . . and just walk. But she stopped, picked up the pail and headed for the henhouse. For her, this was the worst ten minutes of each day—the chore she despised arriving with the early morning sun which she adored.

As she gathered the eggs, she counted reasons to hate chickens—beyond the obvious stink and the filth.

One . . . "sitting hens." The hens who do not give up their eggs willingly, and instead peck and attack when you reach under them to retrieve the eggs.

Two . . . "nasty" surprises. The squashy, gelatinous moments when your hand unexpectedly encounters a warm, freshly laid egg with no shell.

Three . . . chicks and thunderstorms. Running outside in the thunder, lightning and pelting rain to comfort stupid baby chicks who, in their fear of the rolling of thunder, would huddle together and smother each other to death if someone did not intervene.

Grudgingly, she noted it was a good day for eggs with nearly two dozen eggs filling the pail. Heading for the house, she stopped, looked around and quickly darted to the backside of the henhouse. She carefully chose six of the smallest eggs and placed them in a neat row on the grass. Just this once. Picking them up, one by one, she hurled them powerfully, watching each one hit the henhouse and explode dramatically. She watched intently as the yolks slid down the weathered wood, leaving slimy streaks of sunlight. She looked up at the morning sun, taking a deep, satisfied breath.

With her next breath, she grabbed the hose and cleaned the mess before heading inside to cook breakfast for the family. In the afternoon, she would slip a dime into the egg money jar to offset the loss of the eggs. ■

Photos and Bios

Alan Hotchkiss was born and raised in Albuquerque, New Mexico and attended the Voces Institute in 2005. Currently studying architecture and Spanish at the University of New Mexico, he hopes to see the world, but couldn't imagine living anywhere other than the Southwest. He aspires to be not only an architect and designer, but also a linguist, and to continue to study the language and culture of New Mexico.

Alicia Leger was born and raised in Las Vegas, New Mexico. She enjoys academics, especially the challenge of mathematics and writing. She also enjoys playing piano, downhill skiing, and reading. Her favorite authors are Isabel Allende and Jean Auel. The Voces Program in 2005 gave her confidence to perform in front of peers and helped her to communicate her feelings better.

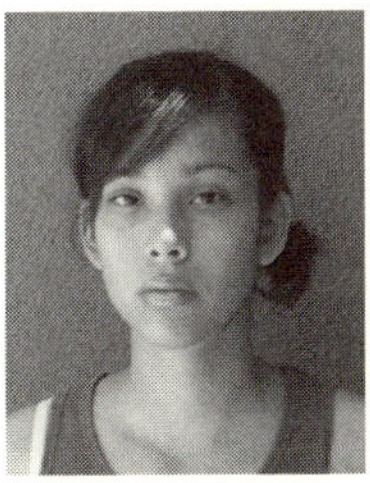

Alyssa Garcia lives in Albuquerque, New Mexico. She was a student in Voces 2006.

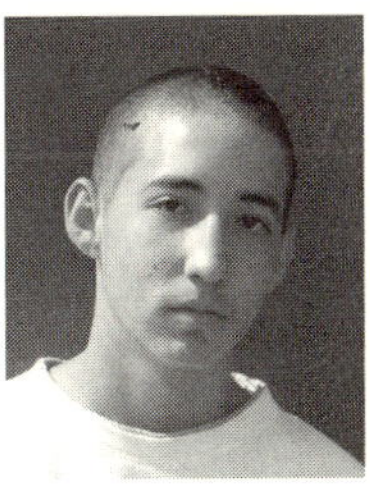

Ambrose Vigil lives in Albuquerque, New Mexico. He was a student in Voces 2002, 2003, and 2004.

Ana Romero was born in Mexico, but now lives in Albuquerque, New Mexico, with her family. She was a student in Voces 2005.

Anisha Imhoff-Kerr lives in Albuquerque, New Mexico. She was a student in Voces 2002 and 2003. Anisha is passionate about writing and sharing her experiences in order to teach others. Since graduating from high school, Anisha has self-published a book about her struggle with depression.

Anthony Roybal lives in Albuquerque, New Mexico. He was a student in Voces 2002.

Anthony "WonderBoy" Alaniz lives in Las Cruces, New Mexico. He was a student in Voces 2006.

Antonio Rael was born and raised in Albuquerque, New Mexico and attended Voces in 2006. He currently attends Amy Biehl Charter High in downtown Albuquerque, where he discovered his talent for and interest in poetry. He is beginning to develop into a slam/performance poet and getting his "stuff" heard throughout the Albuquerque poetry community.

Ashley M. Ellison lives in Albuquerque, New Mexico. She was a student in Voces 2002 and 2003 and now attends the University of New Mexico.

Bianca Lopez was born and raised in Las Cruces, New Mexico and attended Voces in 2006. She has written all her life, but became very involved with writing when she entered a creative writing class in the fall of 2005. With some of her fellow students, she helped organize and host public open mics. She is very grateful for all the opportunities that have been presented to her in her life, including any opportunity to meet writers who love the art as much as she does.

Brittany Jewel lives in Grants, New Mexico. She was a student in Voces 2004.

Carlos Anderson lives in Albuquerque, New Mexico. He was a student in Voces 2003.

Carlos Contreras lives in Albuquerque, New Mexico. He was a student in Voces 2002, worked as the Voces Intern in 2003, and as a writing mentor in 2006. Carlos has continued to write and perform poetry with great commitment and passion. He is a mentor and teacher in school outreach programs. In August 2005, Carlos was a member of the Albuquerque Slam Team that won the National Poetry Slam competition.

Chasity A. Vigil lives in Las Vegas, New Mexico. She was a student in Voces 2004.

Damien Flores hails from Albuquerque, New Mexico. He participated in Voces 2002. He was a member of the 2004 and 2006 ABQ Slam Teams and the 2006 National Champion UNM Slam Team. He has performed across the United States and has been published in the anthology *Earthships: A New Mecca Poetry Collection* by New Mexico Poetry Tangents, *Bomb Magazine*, and *Shine on you Crazy Diamond* by Sunstone Press. His collection of poetry, *A Novena of Mud*, was published by Destructible Heart Press in 2006. He is currently an undergraduate at the University of New Mexico.

Demi Olivas lives in Española, New Mexico. She was a student in Voces 2003, 2004, and 2006 and worked as the Voces Intern in 2005. In addition to poetry, Demi is an accomplished visual artist, working, selling, and showing her pottery in both Albuquerque and Santa Fe.

Egla López lives in Española, New Mexico. She was a student in Voces 2003.

Ehren Salazar-Marcrum lives in Albuquerque, New Mexico. He was a student in Voces 2002 and 2003. In addition to poetry, he creates electronic music and is a recognized visual artist who has been creating, exhibiting, and selling original silk-screen prints since the age of eight.

Elicia Cardenas lives in Albuquerque, New Mexico. She was a student in Voces 2002.

Elissa Hutson lives in Las Cruces, New Mexico. She was a student in Voces 2006

Emilio Juri comes from Argentina and now lives in Albuquerque, New Mexico. He participated in Voces 2005.

Esmé Vaandrager, native Albuquerquean and lover of poetry, art, and romanticism, gets anxious at the thought of writing a biography. She is forever grateful to her family and friends, and gives many thanks to Mikaela and Carlos for making Voces 2006 an inspiring and educational experience.

Faustino Villa lives in Albuquerque, New Mexico. He was a student in Voces 2006.

Felicia Herrera lives in Albuquerque, New Mexico. She was a student in Voces 2003 and now attends Central New Mexico Community College.

Graciela Gonzales lives in Albuquerque, New Mexico. She was a student in Voces 2003 and 2004.

Gregorio Garcia lives in Albuquerque, New Mexico. He was a student in Voces 2004.

Isaiah Baca lives in Albuquerque, New Mexico. He was a student in Voces 2004.

Jasmine Sena lives in Albuquerque, New Mexico. She was a student in Voces in 2002 and 2003 and worked as the Voces Intern in 2004. Jasmine is now an active member of the Albuquerque Poetry Slam community and became Albuquerque's Slam Champion in 2007. She continues to share spoken word poetry through showcases, performances, and slam competitions, the latest at an international competition in Vancouver, Canada.

Jennifer Otero lives in Albuquerque, New Mexico. She was a student in Voces 2004.

Jeremy Maes lives in Albuquerque, New Mexico. He was a student in Voces 2002 and 2003.

Jesse James lives in Albuquerque, New Mexico. He was a student in Voces 2006.

Joe Romero lives in Albuquerque, New Mexico. He was a student in Voces 2006.

Julian Godinez lives in Albuquerque, New Mexico. He was a student in Voces 2005.

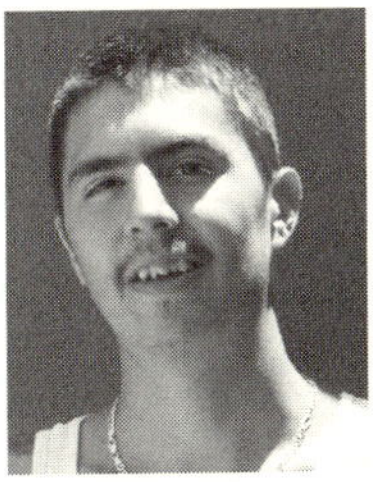

Julio Mendez lives in Albuquerque, New Mexico. He was a student in Voces 2006.

Kaly Thayer lives in Albuquerque, New Mexico and participated in Voces 2004. She has attended special programs for languages, creative writing, and government. She enjoys college and contemplating what she will do with the rest of her life, some options of which are working for the FBI, writing suspense and fantasy novels, or becoming the first female President of the United States.

Kate Twitchell lives in Albuquerque, New Mexico. She was a student in Voces 2002.

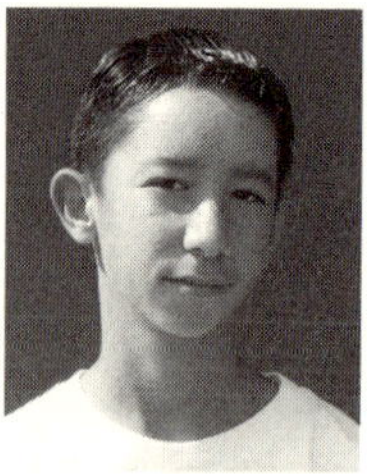

Kevin Pacheco lives in Albuquerque, New Mexico. He was a student in Voces 2002.

Khamyra A. Hall lives in Albuquerque, New Mexico. She was a student in Voces 2002.

Latoya R. Winfield was a student in Voces 2002. She could not be reached to include her work in this anthology.

Lauren Badua lives in Albuquerque, New Mexico. She was a student in Voces 2004.

Lauren Brenner lives in Las Cruces, New Mexico. She was a student in Voces 2006.

Lenell Storey lives in Albuquerque, New Mexico. She was a student in Voces 2006 and now attends the University of New Mexico.

Marcelo Moya lives in Albuquerque, New Mexico. He was a student in Voces 2002 and 2003. Marcelo has always been a passionate artist and started writing poetry when he was in elementary school. The first poems he wrote were intended to be rap love lyrics to impress girls. He has since developed a deeper relationship to poetry, but the subject matter hasn't changed much, just the purpose.

Marisol Servizio lives in Albuquerque, New Mexico. She was a student in Voces 2002.

Martín Montaño-Pilch lives in Albuquerque, New Mexico. He was a student in Voces 2006.

Mary Ferguson lives in Santa Fe, New Mexico. She was a student in Voces 2005.

Matthew Lucero lives in Albuquerque, New Mexico. He was a student in Voces 2002.

Matthew Meyer lives in Albuquerque, New Mexico. He was a student in Voces 2006.

Nakya Ely-West lives in Edgewood, New Mexico. She was a student in Voces 2003 and 2004.

Nick Etre lives in Albuquerque, New Mexico. He was a student in Voces 2005.

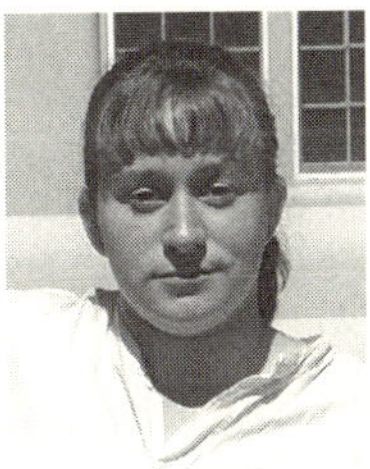

Nikki Poindexter lives in Albuquerque, New Mexico. She was a student in Voces 2003.

Paul S. Hoeg lives in Albuquerque, New Mexico. He was a student in Voces 2004.

Penny Chimal grew up on the Jicarilla Apache Reservation. She was a student in Voces 2003.

Rebecca Ortega lives in Albuquerque, New Mexico. She was a student in Voces 2002.

Revé Chewiwi lives in Albuquerque, New Mexico. She was a student in Voces 2003.

Robert P. Ramirez grew up in Denver and now lives in Albuquerque, New Mexico. He was a student in Voces 2006.

Robyn Ruff-Wagner lives in Albuquerque, New Mexico. She was a student in Voces 2004.

Roxie Ganadonegro came to Voces 2004 from Magdalena, New Mexico. Roxie attended New Mexico Highland University. She could not be reached for permission to include her work in this anthology.

Samantha Emord lives in Albuquerque, New Mexico. She was a student in Voces 2002 and 2003.

Samantha Innis lives in Albuquerque, New Mexico. She was a student in Voces 2003, 2004, 2005, and 2006. She has been passionate about writing since she was ten years old.

Sara Humphreys lives in Albuquerque, New Mexico. She was a student in Voces 2002 and 2003 and now attends the University of New Mexico.

Sara Samani lives in Las Cruces, New Mexico. She was a student in Voces 2006.

Sonja Chacon grew up in Taos, New Mexico. She was a member of two youth teams participating in the National Youth Poetry Slam and a Voces student in 2004. She now lives in Colorado where she is going to college.

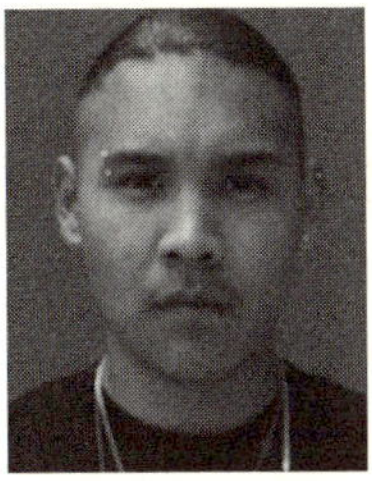

Stephen Juarez lives in Albuquerque, New Mexico. He was a student in Voces 2004.

Tamara Bryan lives in Las Cruces, New Mexico. She was a student in Voces 2004. She now attends the College of Santa Fe and continues to pursue poetry through public performances and personal writing.

Wayne Owens lives in Albuquerque, New Mexico. He was a student in Voces 2006. He could not be reached for permission to include his work in this anthology.

Mikaela Jae Renz has been the mentor for the Voces Program since it began in 2002. Having grown up in Albuquerque, she graduated from the University of New Mexico with a BA in English in 1997 and an MA in Community and Regional Planning (CRP) in 2006. In addition to creative writing, she has taught about community, place, and identity, both in the University Honors and the Community and Regional Planning Programs at UNM. She actively supports spoken word poetry and community-building wherever she can.

Shelle VanEtten-Luaces has been the Director of Education at the National Hispanic Cultural Center in Albuquerque, New Mexico, since 2002. She holds a PhD in education from the University of New Mexico along with twenty years of experience in education that includes public schools, universities, teacher training, distance education, and private tutoring. She is committed to arts and cultural education with special attention to collaborative programs, building community connections, and celebrating the power of individual creativity in daily life.

Afterword

Shelle VanEtten-Luaces

I love the first Monday of June when Voces students arrive at the National Hispanic Cultural Center—always so serious and quiet—on the first day. By the end of the month, the theatres here are their private stages, they know every place on campus to find shade, and their voices echo down almost every hallway.

During these four powerful weeks in June, I watch from the background, listening to the words, the thoughts, the joking, the laughing, and the constant learning. As I watch each group, I remember how amazing it was to be a teenager—and I remember why I am so glad I never have to be a teenager again.

I enjoy the flow of poets, writers, artists, and mentors as they share and teach. I observe as unlikely friendships form and talented leaders step forward. Shy teens find their courage to speak loudly and confidently from a stage—to peers, mentors, and adults. Individuals' voices emerge, and the group listens to all the voices that surround it.

Students share ideas, discuss and critique each other's work, and learn about each other's cultures and families even as they learn to trust the members of the group. Over a month-long conversation, these students mirror an acceptance and celebration of diversity that all communities could stand to strengthen.

Voces continues beyond June. Many students participate for two or three summers. Over time, students become mentors and visiting instructors. Students teach poetry in schools, lead poetry in the community, and perform alongside poets who were once their teachers. Each summer, their poetry becomes a book that we share around the country. Now, those books are a published anthology at UNM Press. The cycle and impact continues as the Voces community grows.

Voces grew and developed under the care, attention, and dedication of writing mentor Mikaela Jae Renz. Voces succeeds when parents and teachers encourage and cajole youth to apply and attend. Voces draws power from the talented and diverse poets, writers, and artists who teach each summer. Voces soars with each student who participates and creates with dedication and commitment. In the end, the list of thank-yous would outnumber the pages of this book. I offer this book and its contents as a tangible thank-you and evidence of the incredible creativity and work of every individual who has contributed to the Voces Writing Institute over the years.

I have enjoyed and learned from each and every voice. ■

Acknowledgments

The National Hispanic Cultural Center (NHCC) first presented Voces: Writing Institute for Youth in the summer of 2002, and it has continued every June under the leadership of Dr. Shelle VanEtten-Luaces.

Voces continues due to the fundraising efforts of the National Hispanic Cultural Center Foundation and generous funders over the years: Sandia National Laboratories/ Lockheed Martin, the Witter Bynner Foundation, American Express, First Data Western Union, and Dr. Tobias Duran, director of the University of New Mexico Center for Regional Studies.

Voces has been supported over the years by the entire staff of the NHCC and the NHCC Foundation with special attention from: Jorge Andrade, Clara Apodaca, Cherie Austin, Thomas Chávez, Andrew Connors, Catherine Jaramillo, Heather Norfleet, Elsa Menéndez, David Sánchez, and Joseph A. Wasson Jr.

Michele Carter at Tricycle Creative has provided design, layout, and formatting for each Voces book—and always done it with such care and genuine appreciation for each page of original writing.

V. B. Price, always a supporter of creativity, community, and poetry, helped make this anthology a reality.

And finally, to the readers. Your willingness to read, listen, and honor these young voices gives this book a place and purpose.